Kaffe Fassett's

Glorious Inspiration

for Needlepoint & Knitting

Kaffe Fassett's
Glorious Inspiration
for Needlepoint & Knitting

Sterling Publishing Co., Inc.
New York

This book is dedicated to Rory Mitchell whose
very real friendship was an inspiration

Opposite title page: *Peacock and Rabbits in a Landscape* by
Pieter Casteels (1684–1749); oil on canvas.
Title page: Needlepoint in progress, *Peacock* by Kaffe Fassett,
worked in tent stitch with wool yards on 10-mesh canvas, 1900.

Editor: Sally Harding
Designer: Polly Dawes
Picture Researcher: Mary Jane Gibson
Artwork: Sally Holmes

Library of Congress Cataloging-in-Publication Data Available

10   9   8   7   6   5   4   3   2   1

Published by Sterling Publishing Company, Inc.
387 Park Avenue South, New York, N.Y. 10016
First published in 1991 in the United Kingdom
under the title *Glorious Inspiration* by Century Editions
Random House, 20 Vauxhall Bridge Road, London, SW1V 2SA
Text and original needlepoint and knitting designs © 1991 by Kaffe Fassett
Distributed in Canada by Sterling Publishing
℅ Canadian Manda Group, One Atlantic Avenue, Suite 105
Toronto, Ontario, Canada M6K 3E7
Printed in China
All rights reserved

Sterling ISBN 0-8069-5887-1

Contents

Introduction

At last I am able to bring you the book I have looked for all my designing life. When working on design projects I have searched book shops, old magazines and museum postcard racks to find good source material for printed fabric designs, needlepoint or knitting ideas. As I staggered home with armloads of books and magazines, each usually containing only a few usable ideas, I dreamt of a single volume that had magically collected together multiple choices of each subject I required. A book that would start the mind adventuring down many creative paths each time it was browsed through.

Though this book was conceived primarily to help needlepoint designers find good sources to stitch from, there is a rich array of colour throughout – from the subtle, faded tones of old shells and ancient tapestries to the bold brilliance of marble inlays and brightly painted flowers – that should supply fresh colour ideas for knitters as well as textile designers. Even though I have already interpreted a selection of the sources (see kit information, page 191), this should not stop you from creating your *own* interpretations.

Every one of us has the ability to create personal and warm-hearted decoration if we can only relax and let our confidence grow. A lot of my courage to have a go at designing comes from surveying the history of decorative art which every culture is rich in. You will be amazed when you realize that so much detailed and finely coloured work has been done by uneducated

Kaffe Fassett working on the *Country Garden Tapestry* needlepoint.

Cauliflower by Basil Smith, watercolour from 'Food from your Garden', *Reader's Digest*, 1977.

Vegetables and Fruit by Christian Berents (1658-1720), oil; Galleria Nazionale di Arte Antica, Rome.

Partially Opened Melon and a Slice of Watermelon by Giovanna Garzoni (1600-1670), tempera on parchment; Palatine Gallery, Florence.

hands. My own art training was less than a year, so I am definitely one who draws inspiration from 'primitive' art and uses details from all of the world's art treasures.

When designing a needlepoint chair cover or large hanging it is so exciting to see how a piece of fruit from a certain painting goes with a flower from a seed packet which together sit on a background from a third source. Over the centuries carpet and tapestry weavers, and even painters, have all resorted to the same borrowing of sources in their work.

The *Country Garden Tapestry* (facing page) uses two seventeenth-century paintings (left), two photographs from the magazine *Country Living* and a watercolour (top left) as design sources. The sky came from a Victorian lithograph and the holly-hocks from several Russian paintings.

Because the scale of each embroidered element is so large I used fewer sources than usual in a tapestry. You can see from the sketch (facing page) that I leave a lot of details unsolved until the end when the decision is made on what is still needed. But it is helpful to draw out the bare bones of the design on paper so that the outlines can be easily transferred to the canvas.

One of the common beliefs of many people in these hi-tech times is a conviction that they cannot create a colour scheme and certainly cannot draw. Being an optimistic American I have never accepted this. In many different ways I have proved to my own satis-faction that people are filled with creative ideas that can be wonderfully and personally expressed. All they need is to be encouraged and given a little confidence.

Good drawing comes from the heart and evolves from your enthusiasm for a subject. Cultivate a direct simple line (see sketch right) that describes the outline of the object. Even a wildly distorted shape can have a charm and personality that is very 'telling'. When we look at rag-rugs and peasant art we recognize dogs, flowers and houses even when rendered in the crudest fashion. It is the personal use of colour

Study for Country Garden Tapestry by Kaffe Fassett, watercolour, 1990.

Country Garden Tapestry by Kaffe Fassett, needlepoint worked in long stitch with wool yarns on 8-mesh canvas, 1990.

11

Rose and Ribbon by Kaffe Fassett, needlepoint kit worked in tent stitch with wool yarns on 8-mesh canvas, 1990

them. That is why in this book I have concentrated on many older tapestries and mosaics that reflect this multi-toned detail.

The kind of sources that work best for me usually contain a bold impact on first viewing, then, as one looks closer, the rich colouring and intricate details are revealed. Flicking through this book you will get a good picture of bold outline and complex texture.

It is rare for me to find a source that contains exactly what I require for a design. I almost always want to add further elements to make a bouquet lusher or place an animal on a different background, etc. This is an exciting game as the source material takes on a completely new life when placed in a different setting. Taking the flowers for the *Rose and Ribbon* bouquet (left) from several sources (right) and then placing it on a rich paisley stripe is a case in point. My favourite addition came when the two sides were bordered with winding ribbons taken from a toile de Jouy print (right).

that catches our eye and makes an object a joy to live with.

When it comes to applying colour to a design it is reassuring to discover that you do not need to master any theories or study great tomes. Simply remember how joyous it is to arrange garden flowers, and then gather a 'bouquet' of yarns that 'sing' to start your project. Observing nature or your favourite painting you will usually find that the effects which attract you are created by many shades of colours working together.

Very often, people starting in the design field are timid in their use of colour and therefore end up with flat predictable work in only a few shades. Any flower or butterfly wing or piece of marble contains many subtle shades of each colour which are continually revealed as you look more closely into

Sometimes I look for a simple background that will show off my foreground object like a jewel. But, more often, I enjoy finding a patterned ground that contains similar elements to my object so that it is echoed or even partially lost in the background texture. When I was working with Steve Lovi on my first four books, for instance, we often looked for a background for knitting and needlepoint that added a whole life of its own — sometimes almost merging with the textile in a camouflage effect. An ex-

Sources for *Rose and Ribbon* needlepoint.

12

er piece differs from most others in
that it is produced by chromolitho-
not hand-coloured — either by the
ishers or by Messrs. Andersen &

ndour out there in the hothouse!
ms rose spreading across the roof,
nder the sun, while beneath them

had
flowe
fallen
beetle, "V
cious they l

, glittering wi
white as p
the
'H

treme example of this can be seen in Thayer's watercolour grouse (page 87).

Contrast is sometimes a powerful effect in design. The roses in the *Autumn Roses* needlepoint (facing page) are so operatic that their vivid differences are enhanced by the deep burgundy and burnt-sienna ground. I enjoyed the way the darkness on the painted glass eased out into tobacco brown, so I kept that in my needle-point rendition.

In fact, I was uncharacteristically true to my source (right) when work-ing this needlepoint, lifting the place-ment and colouring without making many changes or additions. I simply elongated the shapes and let them move out from the centre a bit to make more of a square composition.

Good designing follows no rules; re-maining open to the unexpected is paramount. Until you have tried a par-ticular combination of form or colour you will not know for sure if it works because the most unlikely elements can suddenly spark each other to life. Sometimes a drab object positively demands a luminous-coloured ground, or a bright jewel colour can 'sing' on a neutral one.

Always be prepared to place colours and textures together to see for your-self the effects. Working with colour is not an intellectual game. You should see what the heart feels, that way you will stumble across more and more personal excitement in your work. When in doubt pin up your needle-point or knitting and place colours in the form of wool, or coloured paper,

or fabric near the piece to see if it lifts or distracts from your work.

This book has so many sources for design that I for one cannot wait to use it. In amongst the highly-defined, three-dimensionally-rendered sources in paintings, lithographs, mosaics and textiles, I have placed examples of flat, 'primitive' interpretations that also have great flair. These, more simpli-

Roses painted on glass plate, probably English, circa 1900.

Needlepoint in progress, *Autumn Roses* by Kaffe Fassett, 1990.

14

fied images, are there to encourage one and all to get stuck into designing, in spite of never having done it before.

My primary wish is for you to simply luxuriate in the beauty of the subjects gathered here – to be stimulated by the amazing outpouring of decorative art the world is constantly producing, then to take courage and use the many sources to create your own textiles specifically for *your* heart's desire. Then in years to come a piano stool or sumptuously coloured sweater or a needlepoint carpet you have created will grace the pages of a book similar to this one!

Autumn Roses by Kaffe Fassett, needlepoint kit worked in tent stitch with wool yarns on 10-mesh canvas, 1990.

iero della Francesca's *Madonna and the Egg* (left) has an extraordinary stillness about it. The faces are serious but painted with calm simplicity. Above the heads hangs a dramatic canopy of marble. The Italians with their innate sense of colour have often used marble to striking effect. Placing different patterns and colours of stone in painting-like panels framed in white alabaster is bold indeed. The subtle differences in each panel show up beautifully with this pale separation. Above the panels floats a wondrous shell with an egg suspended on a gold chain. That shell and egg are excitingly sensual shapes for a designer to work from.

By keeping the entire top of the alcove in this delicately pale stone the artist emphasizes the great flared form of the scallop shell. This huge carved shape, half in shadow and half glowing with reflected light, would make a strong detail in needlepoint. It could be elegantly decorative placed on the back of a chair or on a bedhead or on a hanging over a doorway with ropes of other shells hanging down the sides.

For some years, as a young painter, I worked on nothing but white still lifes, mainly of white crockery on draped white cloth. But I also did several compositions of pale shells and eggs and was amazed at how many reflected colours played in their shadows (see my painting of shells on page 37). In this Piero della Francesca shell one can see not only cool blue greys, but warm ochre greens as well as the ivory highlights.

Madonna and the Egg by Piero della Francesca (1410/20-1492), tempera on wood, Italian; Brera Museum, Milan.

The simple, almost mask-like, rendering of the faces would be interesting to attempt in stitches. I have often thought of doing portraits in needlepoint having had so many disasters with painted ones! People rarely like the way they look in oils, but the charming texture of needlepoint might just win over the sitter and their families. Sargent's apt definition of a portrait was 'a painting with something just a little wrong around the mouth'.

Part of the awe we feel when we encounter the brilliant colours of minerals is that such an astounding variety of tone is buried under foot. I was going to say 'in common earth', but hesitated, remembering the vast assortment of colours and textures that earth comes in. From white sandy beaches to red deserts, to black peat, the soil on this planet is anything but 'common'. Still we delight even more in the gemstone quality of minerals: vivid blues, lemons, reds, and emerald greens. I used to love highly valued gems like rubies, diamonds and emeralds, but now gravitate towards the less rare agates and semiprecious stones with their extraordinary complexity of greys, pinks and beiges. Imperfections trapped in these 'frozen' stones are endlessly intriguing to the eye. The medieval use of hefty stones in jewellery, and on objects, displays wonder-

fully these more earthy colourings (see Spanish agate box below).

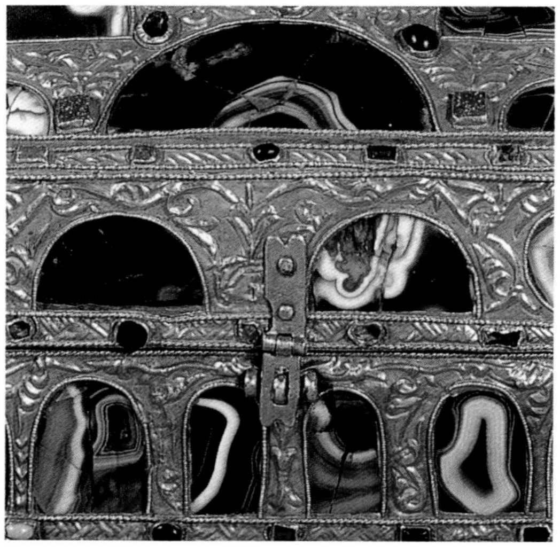

The way marble was arranged in ancient mosques and palaces is wonderfully dramatic. Huge swirling patterns in slabs of bold marble have such a feeling of celebration. We are lucky so many are still dotted throughout the Middle East to inspire us.

Shown here are just four samples of the millions of patterns and colours minerals appear in (facing page). The rhodochrosite, with its luscious watermelon-pinks, is an early stone favourite which I first saw at the British Museum of Natural History. When I arrived in London in 1964 I kept a postcard of it on my wall to cheer me up. It has never appeared in one of my needlepoints, but will certainly be used as a background to something one day. There are at least a dozen pinks, beiges, and smokey tones, plus a few golds in it.

The malachite with shots of blue azurite is a flamboyant display of colour. It is interesting to see in this brilliant green the swelling shapes reminiscent of mushroom growths on trees.

Agate box, Spanish, 11th to 12th century; Oviedo Cathedral, Spain.

Facing page

Polished slab of watermelon-pink rhodochrosite from Catamarca, Argentina; British Museum (Natural History), London.

Polished section of green malachite and blue azurite from Marenci, Arizona, USA; British Museum (Natural History), London.

Section of a blue siliceous rock found in Scotland showing the stems of a small fossil plant.

Polarized light micrograph of a thin section of crystalline marble from Carrara, Italy.

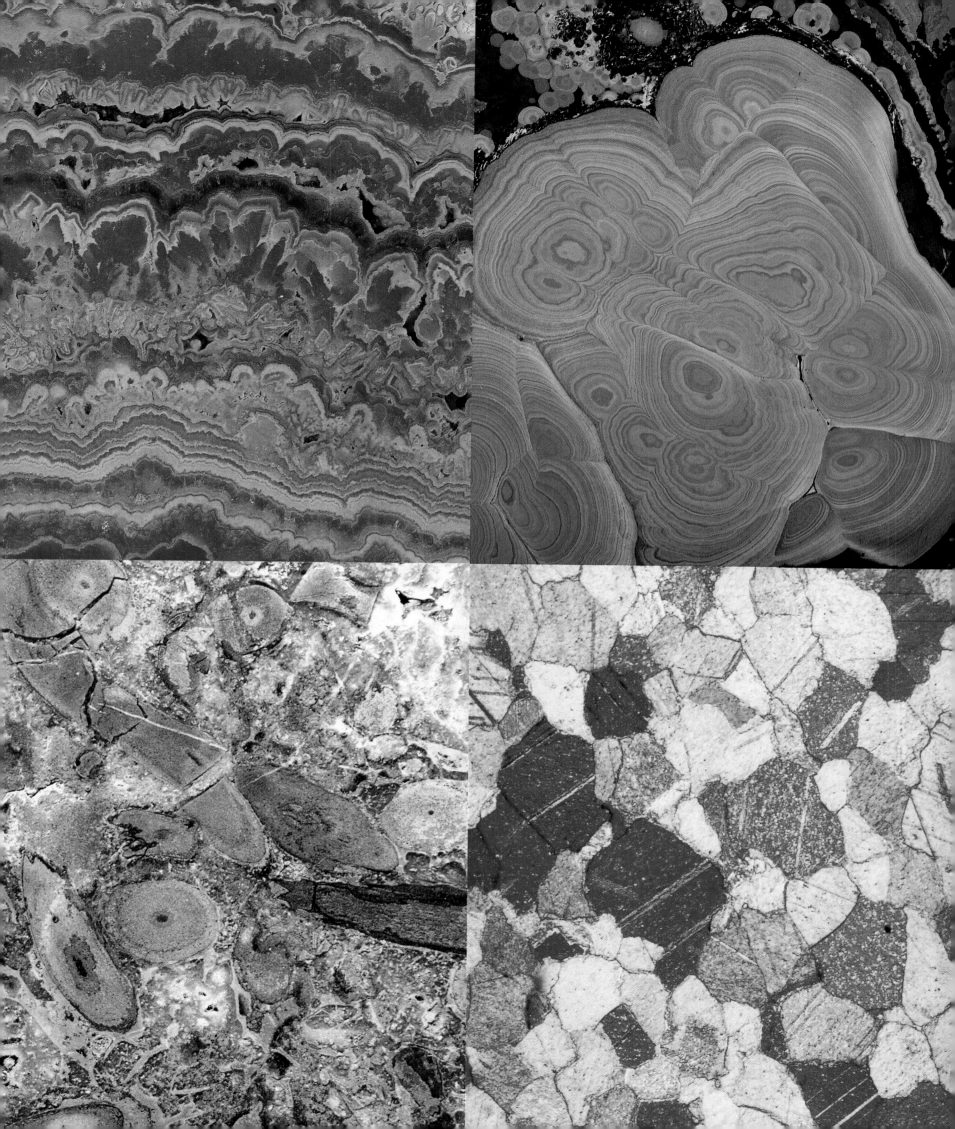

Pages 20 and 21: *Pietre dure* inlaid table with porcelain by Antonia, Italian, 1792; Pitti Palace, Florence.

I once saw an entire room of bright green malachite with lots of gold trim in the Hermitage in Leningrad. I was overwhelmed by its cheering extravagance on a grey Russian day.

The more subtle blue and ochre siliceous rock (page 19) is found in Scotland, a land rich in gorgeous stones. Each time I return to that unspoilt country I am astounded at the beauty of its humblest stone walls.

The crystalline marble (page 19) illustrates yet another of the panoply of patterns that the earth serves up. This arrangement of pinks and golden tones would make a joyous knitting pattern if simplified, or all of the subtle pattern markings of dots and stripes could be captured on fine canvas.

A gorgeous folly, the Italian inlaid stone table (pages 20 and 21) is made up of many types of stones cut into a mosaic. The light glowing on the inside of a bowl is beautifully caught in this unlikely medium. A lively contrast has been achieved between the solid upright cityscape of pots and the organic sprawl of flowers and leaves.

This would be a marvellous model for a collage project. Cutout magazine photos could be used to emulate the rich arrangement of the stone pieces. I once made a 'tumbling blocks' collage entirely with photos of flesh using the

varying shades to create a three-dimensional effect. The finished work looked a lot like marble.

The vibrant colour and the subtle shading within some of the stones makes this *pietre dure* composition a joy to study hour upon hour. The key to the vitality of the design is, as always, the wide range of colours in each group. The warm tones include pinks, reds, ochres, golds, terracottas and fiery oranges. Then come intense blues, greens, cool shadow tones, and a dull lavender maroon on the central flower.

This Italian sixteenth-century tapestry (facing page) is the sort of work that brings me to my knees with admiration and delight. I am not so excited by the story it is telling as I am bowled over by the splendid details it contains. I have not only looked closely at it on many occasions but have incorporated areas of it into a needlepoint (page 183).

An astounding *tour de force* is the depicting of marble in the woven textile. Artisans train for months, even years, to learn how to simulate marble with paint. To create the random vagaries of line and texture and all the subtle colouring of marble in a woven medium·is brilliant indeed.

After viewing marble and other stones arranged in figurative floral

Overleaf

Tapestry illustrating the story of Joseph, after a cartoon by Bronzino, Florentine Medici factory, mid-16th century; Palazzo Vecchio, Florence.

Inlaid marble table top of random curved shapes, Italian, early 19th century.

Tumbling Blocks Sweater by Kaffe Fassett, knitting kit (see page 191 for kit information and suppliers' addresses), wool yarns, 1988.

Inlaid stone table of 'tumbling blocks', Italian, 18th century.

Inlaid stone table in a patchwork of simple squares of varying rich colours and markings, Italian, 18th century.

Inlaid stone table of interlaced ovals and circles, Italian, 18th century.

Cut and inlaid (*opus sectile*) marble floor from a Byzantine palace, 9th to 11th century; Museum of Mosaics, Istanbul.

Marble Blocks Sweater by Kaffe Fassett, knitting kit, wool yarns, 1990.

Detail of a multicoloured marble and cosmati style mosaic floor, Italian, 11th to 12th century; St. Nicola, Bari, Italy.

forms, you will enjoy the bold simplicity of the geometrics in these tables and floors (pages 24 and 25).

When a simple 'tumbling blocks' pattern or chequerboard is done in richly varied and veined stone it displays an unexpected animation. I have been so taken by the classic 'tumbling blocks' pattern, which I first came across in ancient Pompeii and saw later on quilts and parquet flooring, that I tried it in knitting (bottom left, page 24). The stone version of this pattern (top right, page 24) illustrates how amazingly different it looks with the addition of yellow, black, and white outlines around the parallelograms.

The Turkish Byzantine floor (bottom left, page 25) with its quietly alive colours also translated beautifully into knitting (top right, page 25).

The sixteenth-century painting of two figures on the 'landscape stone' (right) turns the flat surface into a vast underhanging cliff. Turned up the other way the stone could even suggest a cityscape in the deserts of Morocco.

The colours in this piece have a remarkable glow for such seemingly sludgy tones – light appears to pour out of the pale beiges. Those smears of muddy green are very rich next to the minky browns. The figures are painted in handsome colours that lift them from the rock without being too disruptive an element. The effect which gives the stone the electric drama it possesses is the underlining of its palest areas with the darkest brown 'shadows', making it look infinitely three-dimensional.

Andromeda by Francesco Napoletano, oil on 'landscape stone', Italian, 16th century; Opificio delle Pietre Dure, Florence.

The 'landscape stone' also has the feel of layers of rags which excite me into wanting to try it as a needlepoint chair cover one day. I like the idea of a new chair which looks as though it is falling into shreds – decay having always attracted me. When I once commented on the ancient shredded drapes in a grand English country house, I was told they would cost a fortune to replace. I said, 'But I love them as they are!' 'So do I!' confided my hostess. I admire cultures that do not over-restore or do away with past objects the minute they show their age.

What is it about the idea of making something out of an unexpected material that so fascinates our minds? I still gasp with pleasure when I come across a painting made of postage stamps or a decorative frame made of cigarette packets. These paintings (right and left) made of sand and shells have some of that humour and enjoyment about them.

The arrangement of shell flowers with phoney cloth leaves and sprinklings of mica in the background has a sweet delicacy about it. The scaly rows of shells decorating the urn and the simple circular motifs on the frame are all disarmingly naive.

On the other hand, the sand painting betrays a highly skilled creator and has some stunning colour combinations. The entire scene of cool pastels on gunmetal grey is beautifully unusual for a start, but the rendering of dark burnished grapes and plums is outstanding. Those glowing red-reflected light areas on the toned blues is gorgeous on

Still-life of Flowers by Frederick Schweickhardt, sand picture, 1803.

all that grey. The peaches are so soft that you could stroke them and the pale green grapes rise to a tingling highlight. The dusty pinks and sage greens quietly complement the rest and leave one stupefied as to how it could all have been achieved in sand!

This is a superb colour scheme for a restrainedly rich needlepoint which could easily influence a whole room's colouring. You could apply this muted, harmonious set of tones to many subjects in this book and use the resulting needlepoint to impart a soft misty quality to a room. The first thing to notice when attempting this

Picture depicting bouquet of flowers, made from small shells, English, 19th century.

would be that the lightest 'whites' are really pale blue. A hard clean white would throw the mood into something else entirely. Also, the 'blacks' are deepest green or charcoal. When analysing colours it is important to get the lightest and darkest sorted out as a short cut to success in mimicking the effect of those colours.

Treasures of the Sea by Jacopo Zucchi (facing page) is a revelry with shells. It takes me back to my childhood on Californian beaches where I made sandcastles and used shells and pebbles to decorate bas-relief statues in the

Seashells from F.M. Regenfuss's *Choix de Coquillages et de Crustacés*, hand-coloured copper engraving, 1758; Linnean Society, London.

sand. Zucchi's figures luxuriating in the beauty of mother-of-pearl and coral display a lively playfulness. The elegant madame swimming ashore, clutching a crayfish and wearing a pearl and coral tiara, looks like she is dressed for the ball, and the fellow using the oyster shell to cover his behind makes me chuckle.

Dressing up in the spoils of the sea, the monkey is having as much fun as anyone. He would figure beautifully as a detail in a still life of tropical fruit or up a flowering tree.

The delicately hand-painted eighteenth-century engraving (left) contains excellent models for the needlepoint designer. We can see here that shells often come in deep and vivid colours, but my preference is still for the sandy colourings and faded patterns.

Balthasar van der Ast's *A Vase of Flowers with Shells in a Niche* (page 32) is a lovely example of such faded patterns on shells, which are here emerging from dramatic shadows. The stripes on the tulips match the shells' strong patterns. The iris at the top of the composition has one of my favourite flower colourings – a bit like decaying leaves or old water-stained parchment.

For superbly upbeat colouring the tawny orangey shades of the Antoine Berjon still life (page 33) is a heart-warmer on a cold day! It radiates a husky warmth that practically fans into flame the high scarlet interior of that pure ivory white shell.

For an excellent way to arrange shells for a needlepoint frame or the

Treasures of the Sea by Jacopo Zucchi (1541-1589), oil on copper; Galleria Borghese, Rome.

A Still Life of Seashells by Antoine Berjon (1754–1843), oil.

A Vase of Flowers with Shells in a Niche by Balthasar van der Ast (circa 1590–1656), oil and pastel.

border to a cushion, the handsome monochrome tray (right) is spot on. It is seductive and strong in just two colours, but imagine the abstract leafy pattern and the overlapping flat shell forms as a carpet border in shell tones and markings.

With its bulbous and pointed shapes crammed together and bursting with energy, Jan van Kessel's bower of shells (following pages) is definitely a celebration of life! I first saw this extravaganza of shells in a black and white book and studied it for months, imbuing it with my own colourings. In my imagination it was all dusty cool pinks, lavenders, and minky beiges.

Tray decorated with shells and seaweed in gold on a black ground, Tôleware, English, early 19th century.

33

Pages 34 and 35: *Shells* by Jan van Kessel (1626-1679), oil on copper.

An early still life of shells by Kaffe Fassett, acrylic on canvas, 1975.

Detail of Kaffe Fassett's *Shells* tapestry, illustrating cartoon of tapestry.

Imagine my shock when seeing this highly coloured, mostly orangey-yellow, arrangement!

Some time ago I was approached by the Edinburgh Tapestry studio to design a large woven tapestry. The first idea that occurred to me was to make something which would work in a large public interior. Shells laid out like Oriental temples seemed a good solution, so I arranged a tray of shells gathered on a Folkestone beach.

When I began to paint them, I deliberately left areas of the work unfinished to encourage interpretation by the weaver. This type of collaboration, sharing insights with a 'co-creator', seems to happen so much more in the world of textiles than in the world of painting.

Shells designed by Kaffe Fassett, tapestry being woven at Edinburgh Tapestry Co. Ltd., Edinburgh, Scotland, 1990.

From the first woven test piece (left) I can see that it is going to be an exciting project. The end result will be a good luminous series of shapes that should hang well in a room with strong architectural details.

2 CHAPTER Sea World

S ailing over its depths, I have a respectful fear of the sea – wondering at all the creatures and plant life that inhabit this deep, watery world. A swim in the sea and long shell-hunting strolls have often left me nurtured and restored.

In this chapter, fish, with bold markings, articulate forms or interesting colourings, and many other treasures have been gathered together. This opening portrait of the sea (right) has a strong clear outline with bags of atmosphere which has been created by the use of all those bluey greys. What a lively movement those great chandeliers of spray give the painting! Each wave has a light top stripe, and the deeper blue-grey stripes under it are repeated in a geometric progression. There is so much variation of size and shape in these scallops that they generate an energy which is astounding for such a methodically formalized composition.

The first few times I studied this painting, I did not notice the two green turtles sitting on the rocks. Hidden details like this, which reveal themselves gradually, add a subtle complexity to a work.

Many times I have toyed with the idea of designing a screen like this one. It would make a handsome needlepoint project for the more ambitious amongst you, perhaps as a background for an arrangement of shells. If you do decide to work from this painting, it is important to notice that the gold background for the scene appears to be one colour, but its metallic quality gives it

A screen in sumi, colour and gofun on a gold ground with breaking waves and whirlpools, Japanese, 19th century.

Red Fish by Kaffe Fassett and Elian McCready, needlepoint worked in tent stitch with wool yarns on 10-mesh canvas, 1990.

Chinese textile with stylized waves (see page 51), which was hanging on my wall, seemed just the thing.

After drawing out the design I had it stitched up in my studio (left). Because the canvas had been drawn on with a non-waterproof blue pen, the blue bled when the work was dampened for stretching. This tinted all the white areas to a pale blue, but like many accidents it actually improved the design. The white areas on the waves and stripes had made the background a little too sharp for the more subdued fish. Now that the contrast has been softened, the background stays at the back and the fish quite happily takes the foreground.

The strong geometric border on this tent stitch needlepoint could work on many different designs. The waves could be replaced with leaves for a flower subject, or with small houses or hills for an animal subject. These stripes are also easy to adjust to any colour scheme by starting with a dark, rich colour and continuing with

a subtle range of tones that harmonize richly with the rest of the painting.

Backgrounds are a danger area when you are trying to keep a design lively. Often a solid colour in needlepoint can stultify a piece. One-colour grounds in deep colours can work quite well, but more often it is better to break them up with tones of colour or a sprinkling of dots. Sometimes the solution for a background is to shade it subtly from one colour to another, or to a more intense shade of itself. This is an effect you will often find in Japanese prints.

It was the blush of orangey reds that attracted me to the seventeenth-century *Dentex Fish* by Jacopo Ligozzi (top left, facing page). He looks quite handsome on a plain paper ground; but being one for a touch of embellishment wherever possible, I looked about for a watery world to place him in. A silk

Facing page

Sparus Dentex or *Dentex Fish* by Jacopo Ligozzi (1547–circa 1632), illustration of fish with red belly, tempera on paper; Uffizi, Florence.

The Telescope from Marius Elieser Bloch's *Ichthyologie*, hand-coloured engraving, 1795; Linnean Society, London.

Worm Parrot from John Whitchurch Bennett's *Fishes of Ceylon*, hand-coloured engraving, 1830; Linnean Society, London.

Flower Parrot from John Whitchurch Bennett's *Fishes of Ceylon*, hand-coloured engraving, 1830; Linnean Society, London.

Rattoo Girawah from John Whitchurch Bennett's *Fishes of Ceylon*, hand-coloured engraving, 1830; Linnean Society, London.

Brindled Grouper from Francis Day's *The Fishes of Malabar*, hand-coloured lithograph, 1865; Linnean Society, London.

Great Red Fire from John Whitchurch Bennett's *Fishes of Ceylon*, hand-coloured engraving, 1830; Linnean Society, London.

Squirrel Parrot from John Whitchurch Bennett's *Fishes of Ceylon*, hand-coloured engraving, 1830; Linnean Society, London.

CYPRIN. MACROPHTHAL.
Das Glotzauge.
Le Telescope.
The Telescope.

PLATE I.

Gestochen auf Kosten des Herrn H. E. zu G.

Fig 1.

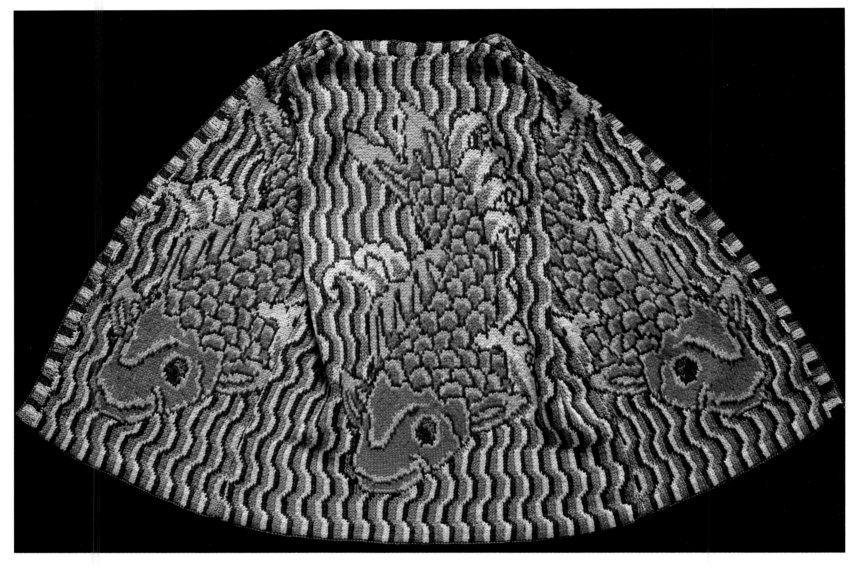

lighter and lighter shades until a pale cream or white is reached.

Recently, I went snorkling in Hawaii and was shocked by the amazing variety of coloured markings on fish. Some of that bold beauty can be seen in the flamboyant colour and pronounced patterns on the fish on page 41.

The luminous glass-like quality of the monstrous fish in Jan van Kessel's painting (pages 42 and 43) is truly captivating. Reflective surfaces usually have a mysterious play of colours that make us reach for obscure colour combinations to try to reproduce them.

Even if it is far from accurate, the abstraction that occurs in attempts to catch a reflection of colour is almost without fail interesting to the eye. There is a lot of drama here in the high contrast of yellow and black eyes, minky browns and silvers on the fish skins, and brilliant gold on the turtles.

Van Kessel's sapphire-blue sky melting into the teal-blue sea should inspire some of you to gorgeous flights of colour stitching. The landscape and sea with the hazy castellated town would make a romantic setting for many other subjects in this book. The

Previous page: The Day's Catch on the Seashore by Jan van Kessel (1626–1679), oil on canvas.

Fish and Waves Waist-coat by Kaffe Fassett, knitting kit, wool and cotton yarns, 1989.

way the sea and sky are painted is quite straightforward to translate into stitches. The clear bright blue fading to white then to clear aqua and on into deeper murkier tones of grey greens could be a *tour de force* in needlepoint.

To me this Japanese tattoo (right) is the culmination of two fascinating worlds – the Oriental rendering of fish in their audacious simplicity and the tattooed body. As a child in San Francisco, I often thrilled at the sight of fish kites in every scale, from tiny minnows to huge man-sized giants, which were often hung from Chinese front porches after the birth of a boy. Superb Oriental fish can also be seen on Eastern porcelain and in Japanese woodcuts with their overlapping scales and fluid fins which seem to float through their allotted space with startling realism.

Tattoos do not have a very elegant image in the West but they are considered an art form in Japan where highly tattooed individuals are 'national treasures'. It always intrigues me when anyone takes such care to have his or her own body decorated. What do you decide to have as a permanent record on your body and why? The idea of a pattern or design wrapped around a body is not, I suppose, that different from wearing a highly patterned knitted garment.

These tattooed waves swirl around the figure so handsomely and the fish is so strong that I was tempted to knit him into a waistcoat (left). I chose softer colours in a wool and cotton mix yarn and worked a repeating-wave

Carp from *The Japanese Tattoo* by Sandi Fellman, 1986.

Mosaic of sea animals, Roman, 2nd century; National Museum, Naples.

ground. The knitting could be even more excitingly rendered by using the same fish but by surrounding it with more dynamic, roaring waves as in the tattoo. Of course, the colours could be changed to brighter ones, or even more subdued ones – such as shades of grey or sepia. The great swirl over the forearm and the splash around the belly button would also be very effective in knitting.

I heartily recommend Sandi Fellman's book on Japanese tattoos which contains, aside from this stunning fish design, many tattoos that would make fascinating all over flower and figure patterns.

What is it about Roman mosaics that is so timelessly appealing? Perhaps it is having to make a picture from millions of glass fragments that brings out a gutsiness in the mosaic artist. The fish in the mosaic above cavort with great vigour and beauty, appearing as detailed and realistic as a painting despite having been simplified and

Sea Animals by Kaffe
Fassett and Caroline
Robins, needlepoint
worked in tent stitch
with wool yarns on
10-mesh canvas, 1990.

stylized by the very limitations of the medium. The most attractive aspect of the composition is, of course, the delicacy of colour; that washy, duck-egg blue sky and dark, teal sea are the perfect ground for silver, ochre and rust fishes.

After I had drawn it out on the canvas, my assistant, Caroline, stitched up one of these mosaic fish beautifully (above). She chose to keep the colours faded and earthy, following the original quite closely. The quality of the mosaic pieces was achieved by introducing tiny little flecks of ochres in the background, giving the whole picture a pointillist effect. For a more upbeat setting, the colours of the mosaic could be interpreted in a brighter fashion to heighten the whole design.

It is always stimulating to the designer's imagination to see the same sort of subject in different colour schemes. The Roman mosaic on page 48 has a similar fish to the one pictured on page 46, but it has been done in

handsome browns, beiges and ochres on a black ground. The lively octopus in the centre of this mosaic is so captivating. Wouldn't this cast of characters make a gorgeous rug? A border for the rug could be taken from a mosaic table (pages 24 and 25) or from the Chinese textile on page 51.

I have had many requests for the instructions to my lobster needlepoint which appeared in my book *Glorious Needlepoint*. The lobster is very strik-

ing because it is set on a bold black and white chequerboard shopping bag. Unfortunately it was designed using an unlimited palette of coloured yarns so it is impossible to translate into a needlepoint chart.

However, for those of you intrigued by the possibility of embroidering a similar lobster, here is an even more dramatic source (above) to stitch from. At least eight shades of orange and some deep reds, almost maroons

Mosaic of sea animals, Roman, 2nd century; National Museum, Naples.

Lobster on a Delft Dish by Charles Collins, oil on canvas, 1738; Tate Gallery, London.

49

A pair of powder-blue ground Rouleau vases with catfish, Chinese, Qing Dynasty, 19th century.

Cloisonné enamel pear-shaped vase, circa 1900, Japanese.

(for the shadows), would be needed for the lobster itself. The sharp blue and white plate supporting the fiery body is wonderfully spotlit against the dark brown shelf. Observe all of the velvety shades of ochres and browns in the background.

This brilliantly coloured creature could also figure most excitingly on a brighter coloured ground such as dazzling green leaves, or on a brocade of magenta and maroon. Alternatively the lobster could become a lively focal point by placing it amongst toned-down shells or monotone fish.

The decorative details in my early life are so vivid to me that I cannot imagine growing up in a house without embroidered, or at least patterned, cloths and decorated dishes. Large shallow fish bowls are among my earliest memories. My mother was an ardent admirer of Oriental taste and she gave us our meals on handpainted Chinese fish bowls in bold maroon and blue. No wonder I have been attracted to fish as decoration ever since.

The deep turquoise enamel vase (bottom left) is adorned with some wonderful 'primitive' fish shapes. The black fish with ochre, powder blue and rust markings is a beauty with its crisply outlined scales, fins and markings.

For more graphically detailed fish in delicate colours the two Rouleau vases (top left) are the perfect source. The deep cobalt blue provides a good contrast with the ivory and grass green in the top fish and wine pink and ochre tinting of the lower fish.

Chinese textile with waves, silk brocade, probably late 19th century.

The balancing and juggling of cool colours and warm ones in design is something one learns quickly when one studies good decorative art. It is this careful and inventive juxtaposition of colour that creates, out of only a few colours, a complex sense of vitality. Often colour arrangements that are all cool or all hot tones can look curiously limited and flat, even when dozens of colours are employed. A decorator friend of mine used to say that one always needed a 'kick' colour, by which he meant a colour that flamed the others to life.

The border of the silk Chinese panel above is a good example of the balance between cool and warm tones creating a most intriguing harmony.

The pillars and rolling fish-filled sea of the thirteenth-century mosaic ceiling (pages 52 and 53) are striking in their simplified boldness. It is always useful to note how successful a straightforward formula of stripes can be. The secret to why these striped pillars are so compelling is yet again the use of a wide enough range of colours. What appears at first glance to be two or three repeating stripe colours is, in fact, five or six.

When I come across a tide pool and spot a glassy flower like the one in Haeckel's engraving (page 54), I am breathless with wonder. The inventive

Blue and white leys jar, Xuande, Chinese, early Ming, 15th century.

Pages 52 and 53: *The Journey of the Magi*, mosaic ceiling, Italian, 13th century; Baptistry, Florence.

forms that these carnivorous creatures assume are magical enough, but the astounding colours they come in surpass my wildest imaginings. Delicate pastels, greens and golds, luminous whites, deep pinky lavenders, stripes and dots and frills all abound. To get the full impact of the transparent beauty of these creatures I recommend a visit to any aquarium that has a selection of these wonders.

The fantasy serpent in this Indian miniature (right) has all of the wild drama that an over-sized monster can conjure up. The scarlet sails seem to scream out as the larger than life snake gobbles up a boat full of poor souls. His stylized circular form fits wonderfully on the page, tail draped Q-like over his greedy body. His skin, made of tightly placed rows of spots, is the sort of detailed pattern a designer can fasten on to and use in many ways, for instance as an all over background texture on a needlepoint.

The elegant little patterns on the ship are also worth remembering. Notice how the pistachio-green garments on some of the sailors 'sing' out

A Monstrous Serpent Devouring the Royal Fleet, Indian miniature, 1790.

Sea Anemone from Haeckel's *Kunstformen der Natur*, lithograph, 1899; Linnean Society, London.

of the soft colouring in this miniature. My favourite element here is the crowded sea, studded with fish, which is treated like wallpaper to set the gruesome scene against.

The miniature kingdoms of small creatures, such as insects and many reptiles, have a special allure for the child in us. The exquisite detail of coloured patterns on butterfly wings, lizard backs or snail shells can hold us staring in wonderment. As a tiny element in a layered composition or as the main subject, small creatures are a rich source of decoration.

The great Dutch flower painters often included all manner of creatures crawling around their huge bouquets. Abraham Mignon's *Flowers and Birds in a Cave* (left) has attracted a stunning cast of characters!

This seventeenth-century work is the sort of painting an embroidery designer dreams about – highly detailed subject matter with lots of colour, presented with total clarity. Each detail is so sharp that it appears to be struck by lightning. The flowers and leaves dominate one's first impression in their almost gaudy brilliance, but slowly, as if in a dream, a world of creatures emerges – butterflies, birds, reptiles and insects. A Daliesque snail crawls across a gunmetal-grey rock. Two beautifully coloured lizards and a handsome frog beg to be stitched into a needlepoint. Each blade of grass and flower petal is theatrically lit for easy interpretation.

Often the paintings we design from have many indistinct areas that can be tricky to simplify for needlepoint, but the details in this painting are highly focused throughout. The whole effect puts one in mind of the great Italian

Flowers and Birds in a Cave by Abraham Mignon (1640-1679), oil on canvas; Hessisches Landesmuseum, Darmstadt.

painter Canaletto who worked in an equally precise and telling manner.

Finding all of the creatures lurking in the shadows of Rachel Ruysch's *Fruit and Insects* (facing page) is like a child's game. Those white peaches and pinky-orange plums seem to provide a glow which lights up the rest of the painting. In the faint orange radiance we can pick out two lizards, four moths, any number of grasshoppers and beetles, and a caterpillar. The grapes have a glassy transparency that would be a challenge to catch in needlepoint. It is a joy to stitch leaves rendered in such dramatic light because they seem to come to life as they grow on the canvas.

The star of the show is, undoubtedly, the elegant little lizard. His blue-black skin is dramatically highlighted in silvery tones which define the distinctive patterning. When starting out as an artist decades ago, I adapted this curvy little beast as my signature, often leaving a line drawing of him, complete with spidery little fingers, in guest books during my travels.

Butterflies and moths are probably the most highly decorated little beings of the living world. There are many sumptuous colour combinations in the butterfly world for you to seek out, but I have chosen strong graphic pat-

Detail of *Fruit and Insects* by Rachel Ruysch (1664-1750), oil on canvas; Pitti Palace, Florence.

terns to facilitate translation into decorative designs (page 60).

The chestnut-browns and golds of Jan van Kessel's *Peacock Butterfly* melted wonderfully into the tawny warmth of my *Flowers on Blue Marble* needlepoint (page 183).

On the other hand, the Persian miniature interprets the butterfly with a bold geometric symmetry reminiscent of Indonesian kites. The cobweb colours of the blossoms with brilliant red accents are intriguing.

There is a lovely pastoral billowyness about the water-colour grass-scape with fluttering butterflies by Myles. The scene takes me back to my first impressions of the English landscape – balmy breezes wafting through endless varieties of grasses. Their colours and textures create a subtle world of their own, well worth exploring. For instance, there is a feathery rhubarb-pink grass in Britain which transforms the fields at certain times of the year.

It is always exciting to see how much the beauty of ornament can enhance a functional object. The Swiss snuffbox is a perfect example. The use of dark crisp outlines around the soft smears of colours gives a stylized, yet realistic, effect.

The Reverend F.O. Morris's hand-coloured engraving of butterflies and

Fruit and Insects by Rachel Ruysch (1664-1750), oil on canvas, Pitti Palace, Florence.

caterpillars uses black, white and red in two quite different applications. On one butterfly the white spots on black create a dark elegant feeling, while on another the dark red and black fashions a brighter, fresher projection. These would make sharp details in design.

It is interesting to see in Huyter's engraving how different the backs and fronts are on some species. The silky blue with strong brown on the front of the butterfly's wings provides a lively contrast with the green gold and pink markings on the back.

The mid-eighteenth-century Italian coffee pot shows how even a pared-down rendering of these delicate creatures reads very well.

On the *Peppered Moth* by Moses Harris, the brilliant splashes of scarlet are exciting, but I am particularly drawn to the bold wood-grain effect of browns and beiges. The shading from light pink, through deep red, makes the colours vibrate, and the dramatic black areas underline this dynamism.

The butterfly from *The Hours of Anne of Brittany* (above) is a wonderful, gutsy specimen to behold! It was drawn in the late fifteenth century when every detail of a painting was

Flowers and Butterfly from *The Hours of Anne of Brittany*, miniature, late 15th century; British Library, London.

made to take on the solidity of stone. I love the articulate depiction of the leaves and flowers and the spontaneous paintwork of the butterfly. You would not need much of an art education to reproduce those simple brushstrokes.

Part of the illusion of the solidity of this painting is created by the strong

Facing page

Detail from *A Peacock Butterfly* by Jan van Kessel (1626-1679), oil on copper; Ashmolean Museum, Oxford.

The Butterflies' Haunt (Dandelions and Thistles) by W. Scott Myles, oil on canvas, 19th century.

Butterflies and Caterpillar by P. Huyter, engraving, 18th century; Chester Beatty Library and Gallery of Oriental Art, Dublin.

Detail from *Bird on a Branch with a Butterfly*, Persian miniature, end of 18th century; Philadelphia Free Library.

Swiss gold and enamel butterfly snuffbox by Rémond, Lamy & Cie, Geneva, circa 1800.

Capodimonte porcelain coffee pot and cover decorated with butterflies and other insects and with gilt motifs, Italian, mid-18th century.

Detail from painting of *Studies of Butterflies and Caterpillars* by James E. Bourhill, watercolour on paper, 1885.

Butterflies and Caterpillars by Revd. F.O. Morris, hand-coloured engraving, 19th century.

Peppered Moth by Moses Harris, book illustration from *The Aurelian*, hand-coloured engraving of butterflies, caterpillars and leaves, 1794.

Picture of vase with flowers made from butterfly wings, English, 19th century.

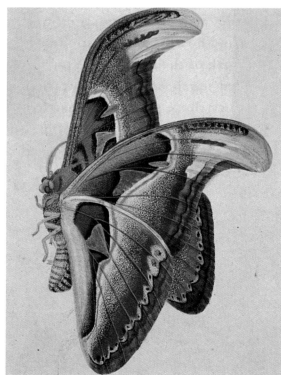

Moth by an anonymous Chinese artist, watercolour, circa 1805; India Office Library, London.

shadow close to each item in the design. This shadowing could be applied to many different subjects in this book to produce a bas-relief effect.

There is little else that couples sensitive subtlety with plucky drama like butterfly and moth wings. The picture on the left is one of the amusingly daft things people make from these gorgeous wings. The tawny colours and the distinct circles created by contrast colours on the wings have a gentle appeal.

How about this Chinese moth (left) for sheer elegant bravado! It is a wonderful lesson in how to use a textured black line to emphasize shapes and intensify colours. Every inch of the wings is covered in shimmering dots, yet they are contained by a bold outline that carries across a great distance. Notice how many shades of browns have been employed – camel tones, chestnut, rich rusts, golden ochres, and delicate pinky beiges. Also, a cool minky brown sits on those centre triangles. By being bordered in a hard black edge, which softens out into the surrounding deep brown, the mink tone is spotlit in a most exciting way. This is a clear visual tip on how a dullish colour can make a strong impression.

The watercolour effect of the artichoke green and lavender *Hawk Moth* by Haserick (facing page) made it a natural choice for tent stitch. My assistant, Jill, stitched the moth on to canvas after I had drawn it on a circle.

There are so many things that could be done with this design. Although I chose a Japanese brocade for the back-

Oleander Hawk Moth by Arthur Augustus Haserick (1862-1937), watercolour; V&A Museum, London.

ground (right), several other equally effective settings spring to mind. Lichen covered stone or even the beautiful mottled bark of a eucalyptus tree would frame the creature beautifully. The moth could even be embroidered in silk on an actual brocade fabric.

Once you have the knack of designing from various sources do not hesitate to try changing the entire palette of your source. The hawk moth, for instance, could be worked in bleached out pastel shades for an almost white look; or it could be rendered in deep gutsy colours on a black or a dark burgundy ground.

Hawk Moth by Kaffe Fassett and Jill Gordon, needlepoint kit worked in tent stitch with wool yarns on 10-mesh canvas, 1990.

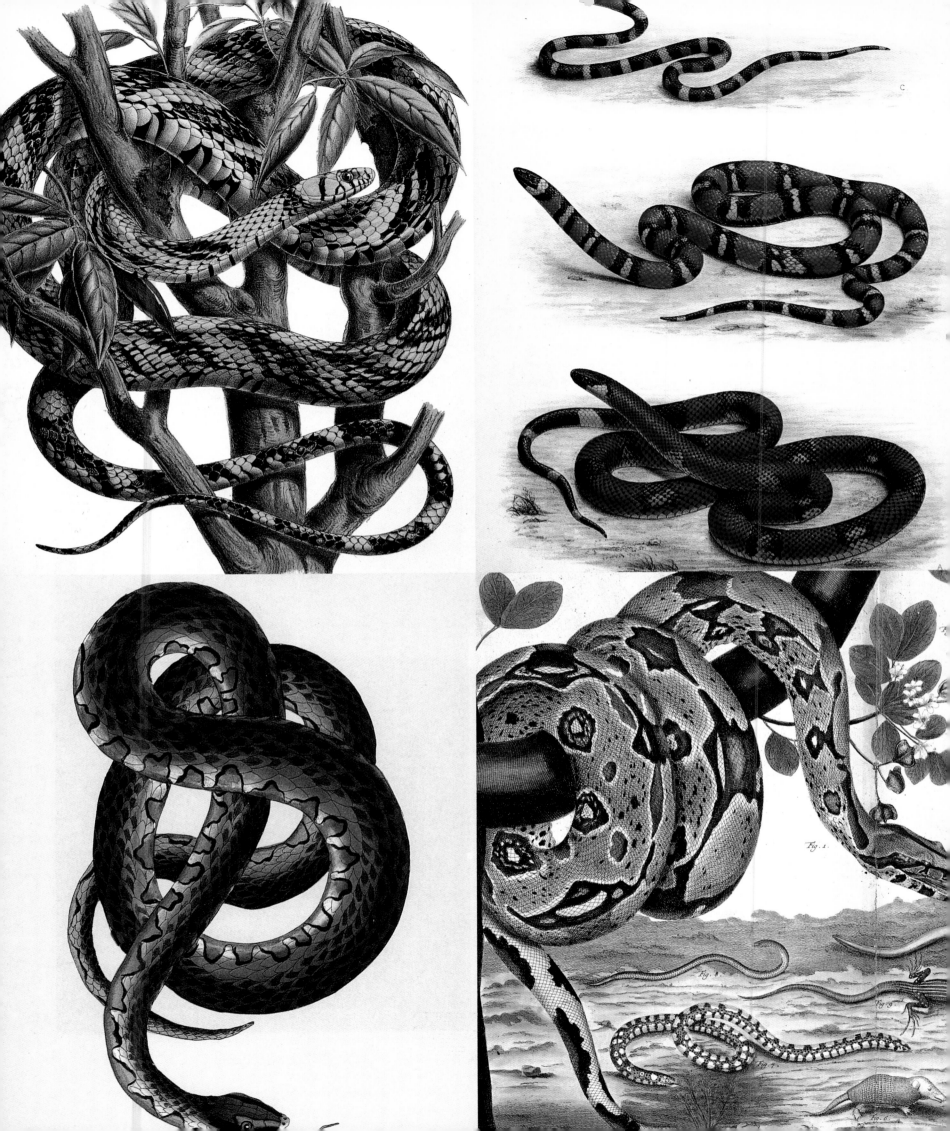

Frontispiece from Roesel von Rosenhof's *Histoire Naturalis Ranarum*, hand-coloured engraving, 1758; Linnean Society, London.

The fashion world discovered snake skin in the 1920s and has never really recovered. It is one of those perennial patterns that keeps cropping up on boots, bags, belts and printed fabrics. When you glance at the mosaic scales on the snakes featured here it is little wonder.

Although the vivid colouring of some reptiles is breathtaking, the greys and browns are equally wonderful to work from. I cannot recall many needlepoint, or embroidered, snake designs, so it is up to us to start using these handsome creatures (facing page) in inventive ways.

The de Morgan tiles (right) are an inspiration. Great S-shaped bodies with

Four-tile panel by William de Morgan, late 19th century.

bold yellow and black markings loop through branches of delicate flowers – all this on a dark turquoise base that makes their grass-green bellies glow handsomely.

Rosenhof's salamander (above), with its intense markings of black and yellow, would be an oppulent addition to a great flower extravaganza or a landscape. Alternatively, imagine him mirror-imaged as a border for a needlepoint, tail-to-tail, nose-to-nose around a mirror frame.

Facing page

Spilotes Salvini from Albert Günther's *Biologia Centrali-Americana*, lithograph, 1885-1902; Linnean Society, London.

Coronella Annulata from Albert Günther's *Biologia Centrali-Americana*, lithograph, 1885-1902; Linnean Society, London.

Blue Snake, illustration from Shaw and Nodder's *Vivarius Naturae* or *The Naturalist's Miscellany*, hand-coloured engraving, 1796-1813.

Snake from Albert Seba's *Locupletissimi Rerum Naturalium*, hand-coloured engraving, circa 1750; British Museum (Natural History), London.

Right: *Lizard* from Maria Sibylle Merian's *Metamorphosis Insectorum Surinamensium*, hand-coloured engraving, 1714; V&A Museum, London.

Below: *Lizard* by Kaffe Fassett and David Forrest, needlepoint panel worked in tent stitch with wool yarns on 8-mesh canvas, 1990.

When I flipped through the material in this book trying to decide which subjects to interpret as needlepoints, this wonderful lizard's coat (below) was my first choice. I drew the curling posture out on a canvas and David, one of my assistants, stitched it in tent stitch on eight-to-the-inch mesh canvas, using the yarn double. A different barren landscape was chosen for the background and the slightly obscured back leg was omitted. It would be interesting to see another version of the design either on a pile of smooth, more patterned, rocks or on a leafy ground.

What is totally delightful about this lizard is the amount of pinks, golds and greens between the patches of brown on his madly-patterned skin. The configurations in brown with washes of paler colours are excellent inspiration for a knitted design. Treat-

ing it as a two-colour a row design, you could do carefully amber shaded stripes of pastels under a series of floating, fragmented dark shapes.

It is amazing how instructive these hand-coloured engravings can be. Many have been included in this 'tome', as their sharp, clear details are easily translated into other designs.

Because I wanted each page of this source book to have a painted, woven, glazed, beaded, or marquetry texture to it, I have omitted straightforward photographs of subjects. Having been fashioned by an artist's hand takes a source one step further towards abstraction and therefore makes it easier to stitch from than it would be from a photographed image. Hopefully you will find that this approach makes successful designing that much simpler.

Frogs come in an astounding array of patterns and colours. The watercolour, the porcelain dish and the sculpted frog (left) show how various artists have interpreted these engaging reptiles. Japanese art is full of extraordinary frogs, some of giant proportions, but I find that simple nature books often contain the best models. The detail from the amazingly bright plate is shown here because of its delightful setting. If I had designed the dish I would have made the frog a brilliant lime green and the generous flower pale or deep pink.

The eighteenth-century Fulda faience frog is perky, and it shows how even the most simplified rendition of a frog is unmistakable. The big yellow feet,

One of a pair of Fulda faience frogs, German, mid-18th century.

Detail of earthenware dish with painted frog on lily, and dragon-flies by J.T. Deck, French, 1865; V&A Museum, London.

Rana Asculanta from Roesel von Rosenhof's *Histoire Naturalis Ranarum*, hand-coloured engraving, 1758; Linnean Society, London.

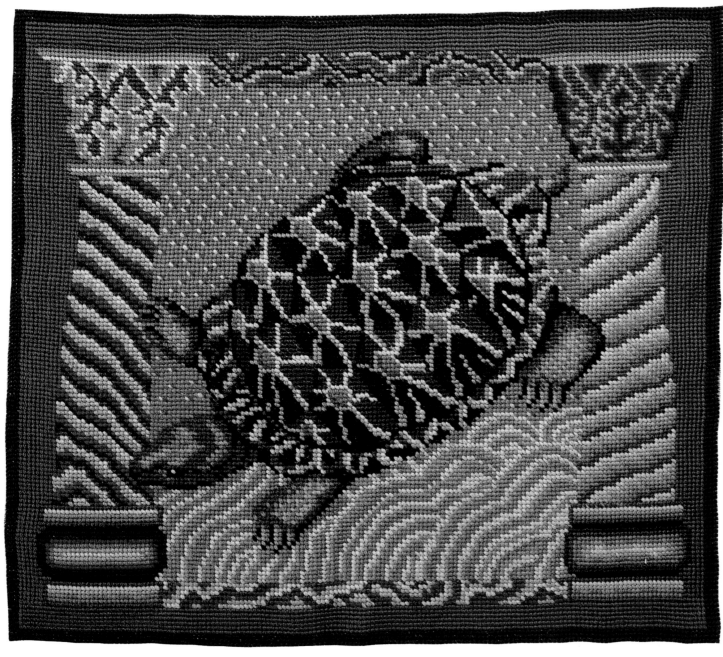

Turtle by Kaffe Fassett and David Forrest, needlepoint kit worked in tent stitch with wool yarns on 10-mesh canvas, 1990.

the bulging eyes and the vivid blue-green and black coat would 'read' in any composition as a 'frog'.

The inspiration for the wonderfully patterned needlepoint turtle crawling down into the water between two bold pillars (above) is taken from a mixture of sources. The muscular engraving from Albert Seba's eighteenth-century opus (pages 70 and 71) was the starting point. The large

Testudo Radiate by Edward Lear, from Bell's *Monograph of the Testudinata*, hand-coloured engraving, 1836–1842; Linnean Society, London.

69

Fig. 6.

Fig. 1.

Fig. 5.

Fig. 3.

Turtles from Albert Seba's *Locupletissimi Rerum Naturalium*, hand-coloured engraving, circa 1750; British Museum (Natural History), London.

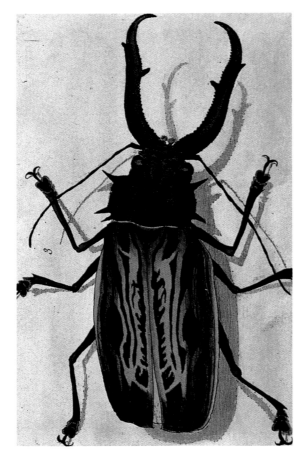

Right: *Beetle* by F.N. Martinet, from Daubenton's *Miscellanea*, hand-coloured engraving, circa 1774; Linnean Society, London.

Below: *Grasshoppers* from Dru Drury's *Illustrations of Natural History*, hand-coloured engraving, 1770-1782; Linnean Society, London.

central turtle was used for the shape of the body and head. Then the star bursts on the turtle in the lower right-hand corner provided the pattern. The two bold pillars and the stylized water came from the mosaic on pages 52 and 53. Fragments of marble lent the finishing touch for the border.

The entire engraving of sundry turtles could be used just as it stands for an amusing carpet idea for a modern room, with leaves and flowers added for an antique interior.

The black and gold side-view of Lear's *Testudo Radiata* (page 69) shows a different characteristic of the turtle. Having seen these reptiles looking quite flat, isn't it amazing to see how bulbous their shapes can get!

If I have not already lost half of my audience with the snakes and lizards, I am sure I will loose some with these dramatic 'creepy crawlies', as the English call them. I know they are nightmarish to behold, but they are in-disputably beautiful.

Beetles are scary enough to see quietly making their way across a room, but downright terrifying flying as in Elias van den Broeck's still life (facing page), where one looks like a new form of fighter plane.

Beetle forms and markings are often stunning and it is little wonder that the Egyptians used them for jewellery. The large ebony beetle in Martinet's engraving displays rich amber-gold patterns (top left) and deep, toasty browns on his sides and head. Imagine him on an enormous purple cabbage — what a cushion that would make!

A Bouquet of Roses, Morning Glory and Hazelnuts on a Ledge, with Grasshoppers, a Stag Beetle and a Lizard by Elias van den Broeck (1650-1708), oil on canvas.

Detail of *Garden Dormouse and Mole* by Jacopo Ligozzi (1547–circa 1632), tempera on paper; Uffizi, Florence.

Gerbils by an anonymous Indian painter, gouache, circa 1805; India Office Library, London.

Grasshoppers with their fan-like wings of brilliant colour are wonderous to watch flying about on a summer's day. Dru Drury's grasshoppers (page 72) could figure marvellously in a huge needlepoint bouquet or in a grass-scape like the one the butterflies flitter across on page 60.

The theatrically lit, late seventeenth-century painting by Elias van den Broeck (page 73) has two stunning grasshoppers - one flying and one sauntering up to feast on a rosebud. This painting also contains excellent references for leaves, sharply-defined flowers and nuts, and a jaunty little black and amber snail.

Many artists have indulged in depicting little furry creatures in seductive detail. The Italian tempera dormouse (above left) was painted by Jacopo Ligozzi in exquisite sharpness. From the tiny pink hands to the bold, inky mask over a sharp eye, to the chic pinky brownish-grey of the coat, this is a superb design subject. Even the

Black Rat Eating Eggs by John James Audubon (1758-1851), oil on canvas; American Museum of Natural History, New York.

walnut meal is treated with the respect allotted to a jewel.

The painting of gerbils (above right) contains that golden warmth of Indian gouaches which are always such a joy to work from. Like the Chinese, Indian artists often convey the essence of their subject in the simplest, most direct manner. The intricate detail in those ears and in every hair is depicted without the gouache looking at all fussy.

Finding this glowing painting of rats (facing page) surprised me. I had never seen Audubon tackle anything but birds. What characteristic energy and life he has imbued these rats with! His rich composition of mellow browns and ambers has great style. The blue black of the dark rat contrasts excitingly with the creamy eggs and pale belly of his neighbour. I am often drawn to tonal compositions like this. At a glance I can see dozens of ochres, honeys, rusty browns, and deep burnt siennas – not to mention the steely blue greys and golden creams.

CHAPTER 4

Wild Animals

Those of us who live most of our lives in cities are often startled by the intense beauty of wild animals. Their wary independence and imminent swift retreats make our perception of them that much more vivid.

After moving from San Francisco to the wild coast, I valued my sightings of cheeky racoons, wild cats, graceful deer and discoveries of animal bones. I wondered at the intense colours of the blue jay or the fascinating forms of various skulls.

What a line of characters (right) appear in this sixteenth-century Flemish tapestry! The faces are really very amusing. Note the glamorously groomed lion and the flying turkeys. All of the birds' dangling legs make a delightful line-up.

Aside from the many animal and reptile forms in the tapestry, the setting itself has many usable elements for needlepoint. Grasses and leaves, a little rolling landscape and stylized, but effective, shadows, all are sharply defined and easy to work from.

A moment's contemplation of big cats explains why artists and craftsmen have been so inspired by them. Though they are powerful in their potential for destruction, these beasts are graceful and elegant in movement. Their great jewel-like eyes fix the viewer with an intense stare, and their markings, whilst bold in outline, contain a mercurial colouring that is entrancing.

John Sargent Noble's painted leopard (page 78) has a luxurious fur

Detail of *Adam Naming the Animals*, Flemish tapestry, 16th century; Accademia, Florence.

Leopardskin Sweater,
by Kaffe Fassett,
knitting kit, wool and
silk yarns, 1990.

which shines out against the muted cell. The leopard spots echo my knitted shades (left) of rich coppery brown fading to a golden cream.

With great simplicity, almost as if creating a caricature, this early Greek mosaic (right) describes the fierceness of a wild beast. The very roughness of the shading and spots can teach those of us who do not have good drawing or painting skills just how it is done. If you have a go at drawing a simple form, do not worry how crude it appears at first because you can always learn to refine the shading and rendering later. Often a first rough attempt at making an outline of your subject will have a liveliness that is lacking in a more finely finished drawing.

Facing page: *Dionysus Riding Leopard,* mosaic, Greek, AD 180; House of Masks, Delos, Greece.

The Leopard by John Sargent Noble (1848–1896), oil on canvas.

Above: Lion rug,
Hamadan, Persian,
early 19th century;
collection Manijeh
and Parviz Tanavoli.

Right: Tiger 'Lion
rug' by Boyer Ahmad
Lori, Persian,
mid-19th century;
collection Manijeh
and Parviz Tanavoli.

Most of these were stylized and very powerful.

The simple, rather flat, handling of these big cats on rugs make them easy subjects for both knitting and needlepoint. Boyer Ahmad Lori's nineteenth-century tiger (bottom left), with feet like bent forks, displays a striking random geometric layout of black on orange. Its little paisley pattern surround would figure marvellously in a knitted pattern.

The lion rug from Hamadan (top left) is probably a better design source for needlepoint. Aren't those luscious flower patterns quite good ideas to use for other backgrounds, perhaps for a needlepoint of a china bowl or a bouquet of flowers or a butterfly? Strong repeats of flowers like this give a good formula for the layout of a design which could be used as the vehicle for any colourway. Those flat lion silhouettes in the border of the lion carpet would make a perfect knitted repeating pattern.

More realistic renderings of lions and tigers can be seen in the two William Huggins paintings (facing page). Both of these animal portraits would make brilliant needlepoints in their different ways. The deep ochre silkiness of the lion is contrasted with all those many shades of gold, platinum and straw in his mane. Huggins' tiger is a veritable ball of orange fire, his great gold eyes daring you to touch his dinner.

An Oriental fantasy of tigers is depicted in the Japanese woodblock print (facing page). Wonderful tawny

About the same time that I designed the knitted leopardskin, two remarkable exhibitions came to London. First a rapturous show of lion carpets was exhibited at the Barbican Gallery where the extraordinary variety of approaches tickled and inspired all who experienced those rooms full of lions. A few of the lions were quite lavishly realistic and surrounded by flowers and other motifs, while the others were expressively 'primitive'. Later the Hayward Gallery on London's Southbank mounted a very handsome show of Tibetan tiger rugs.

Top left: *He Who Dares* by William Huggins (1820-1884), oil on canvas.

Top right: *Tiger's Head* by William Huggins (1820-1884), oil on canvas.

Bottom: *A Dragon and Two Tigers* by Sadahide, woodblock print, Japanese, 1858; V&A Museum, London.

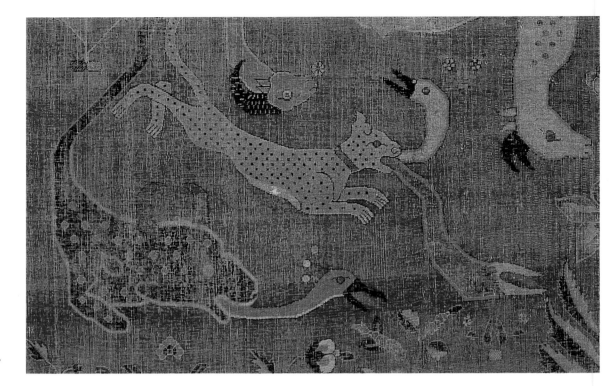

Fragment of grotesque animal carpet, woollen pile, cotton warps and wefts, Mughal, late 16th to early 17th century; The Burrell Collection, Glasgow, Scotland.

Heraldic Dog Sweater by Kaffe Fassett, wool yarns, 1989.

82

shades, and bold stripes running in all directions, make this a strong design source full of lively animation.

The irrepressible movement of animals is often beautifully caught in the decorative arts by the use of simple flat forms. The grotesque animal carpet (facing page) and the beaded picture seen here (below) use graceful, bold outlines filled with dots to express these energetic creatures.

In the seventeenth-century beadwork picture, flowers and trees dominate the animal forms and clear glass beads are used to create an exciting abstract texture. It is interesting to note how detailed, pared-down forms can look in a design if they are depicted in a texture such as beads.

Sharply defined on their terracotta ground, the fanciful dotted animals of the Mughal carpet became the basis for my *Heraldic Dog Sweater* (facing page). Other animal forms which I added to the design came from ancient brocades and embroideries. I filled the spaces between the animals with little green tufts of grass like those found on antique tapestries. The diagonal striped ground had an heraldic air about it, hence its title.

The very fine mosaic with birds (pages 84 and 85) seems to get more beautiful with each viewing. It exem-

Beadwork picture, English, 17th century; the collection at Parham Park, West Sussex, England.

Previous page: *Landscape with Birds* by Marcello Provenzale, mosaic, Italian, early 17th century; Pitti Palace, Florence.

pliifies my edict that even with the subtlest subject matter, masses of colour tones give an inner life to a design. Everything in the foreground is sharply defined, yet so harmonious that its complexity is revealed only on close scrutiny. Shades of brown seem to tie the whole arrangement together; each bird fades from red or yellow into soft browns, and the owl is resplendent in multi-tones of brown. Even the green leaves merge from greens to brown shadows whilst the smoky, ethereal background city all but fades away. These little splinters of coloured glass lend themselves to easy imitations in wool or silk needlepoint tent stitches.

The striking, bold colours of peacocks and parrots are, indeed, compelling; but the subtle colours of tawny owls, ducks and grouse have their own charm. It is astounding how much richness there is in shades of beige, grey, browns and ochres.

The early nineteenth-century British porcelain decorated with feathers (below) has a wonderful, if quiet, life about it. The warm gold and sienna border gives it such a glow. Deliciously detailed, the Indian owl watercolour (below) would make a handsome needlepoint with a border of

Owl, watercolour, Indian, circa 1806; India Office Library, London.

Barr, Flight and Barr porcelain bough pot and pair of vases, British, circa 1810.

Facing page: *Male Ruffed Grouse in the Forest* by Gerald M. Thayer, watercolour on paper, circa 1905; Metropolitan Museum of Art, New York.

feathers from the porcelain. The owl's form is so precisely drawn for the embroiderer, with the minimum of shading to worry about.

The watercolour of the *Male Ruffed Grouse in the Forest* (page 87) draws one into the world of delicate pattern – from the lichen-covered rock to the leaf-strewn ground, to the amazing bird feathers, and on into the intricate branches of the trees. The way the bird nearly loses himself in all of the pattern has a great magical quality for me. I am passionate about the patterns and colours which we see merging in life. By keeping all of the colours so soft and muted, a few elements of the design, like the pale green mossy branch in the lower left corner of the painting and the faded plum leaf in the lower right corner of the painting, really glow.

Parrot Sweater by Kaffe Fassett, knitting kit, wool yarns, 1990.

It is rare in the decorative arts' world to come across a work as lavishly imbued with colours as this glass mosaic (facing page). There are so many rich corners in this work that could supply entire colour scenes in themselves. The bottom half is cool and earthy, with shots of hot golds and magentas, while the top contains tawny peaches and hot lavenders punctuated with icy turquoises. The middle with the creamy birds is a high apricot and terracotta with cool blues and greens.

The first thing to note when working from this source is that there is no white. The lightest tones are sky blue and cream.

Composing a piece with great chunks of colour can lead to a very vigorous work, and for this reason many designers experiment with collage. Ripping up paper to make a colour combination for knitting, or needlepoint or a fabric print, can free the tightness in design that we all suffer from at times. Confirmation that this is a good visual idea comes from seeing fallen leaves of various colours scattered on a pavement: a thrilling sight, particularly when the leaves have been broken up to become more abstract. Stones on a beach give me the same excitement – tones and tones of similar colours containing such subtle variety and texture.

When I first saw this glass mosaic I was moved to use the vibrant colours in some way (see knitting above). I began by just knitting the colours in random areas, but soon found that some quality that the mosaic contained was missing. The physical act of bringing the glass pieces together, while leaving a slight gap, gave the colours a certain clarity. I decided to knit a dark outline which changed slightly in tone as the work pro-

Glass mosaic exhibition piece, traditionally attributed to Joseph Briggs, circa 1900; Haworth Art Gallery, Accrington, England.

4

Parrot by Jacopo Ligozzi (1547–circa 1632), gouache on paper; Uffizi, Florence.

Jacques Baraband's *Red Parrot* (page 91) is a particularly intense character. The bird's saturated redness and its lavender middle make the royal-blue crest of the wing shine out wonderfully. The large black beak and trim blue tail complete the stylish outfit.

The stone mosaic (page 91) is included because of its outstandingly subtle colourings, which would be very attractive in a knitted garment. The stormy greens with burnt oranges and touch of lavender could be used in a simple geometric repeat pattern.

In the de Morgan painting (page 91) you can see how cleverly the grapevine is used to give a strongly structured setting for the big beautiful birds. Both of the darker parrots on page 90, one by Bourhill and one by Dixon, have a shadowy intensity.

The Detmold *Red Macaws* (page 90) inspired my *Red Parrots* needlepoint (page 91). One of my assistants, Elian, worked the birds in long stitch which gives it a definite boldness and feather-like appearance. My first decision was to have a solid pinky-orange background, but, after living with it for a spell, all of us in the studio felt something was lacking. The final harmoniously shaded colours made the birds come into their own.

After the brilliant scarlet of the preceding parrots, the Ligozzi parrot

gressed. The dark frame around each section gave the colours that missing intensity.

For sumptuous reds the parrots on pages 90 and 91 offer you a chance to really indulge in the delight of bright colour. The secret of translating these glowing reds into other designs is to keep the colours as clean as possible. The shadows are deep maroon, not grey or brown, with touches of magenta helping to spark them to life. The luminous blues, lavenders and bright golds give the reds a lift as well.

Previous pages

Two Parrots by Ferdinand Bauer, watercolour, circa 1805; British Museum (Natural History), London.

A White-headed Parrot with Butterflies and Grapes by Samuel Dixon, embossed picture, late 18th century.

A Cockatoo, a Red Vented Parakeet and a Grey Parrot by James E. Bourhill, oil on canvas, 1886.

Red Macaws by Edward Julius Detmold (1883-1957), watercolour on paper of two parrots on a branch.

Red Parrot by Jacques Baraband (1767/8-1809), watercolour and gouache on paper.

Parrot Eating a Cherry, *pietre dure*, Italian, late 18th century; Burghley House, Lincolnshire, England.

Red Parrots by Kaffe Fassett and Elian McCready, needlepoint kit in long stitch, 1990.

Design for a tile panel by William de Morgan, watercolour, circa 1890; V&A Museum, London.

(left) is a sharp contrast. The tawny burnt-orange chest of the bird fading into the mellow gold throat and tail is perfectly framed in blues. What a range of blues they are – from Mediterranean sea aquas through to Gauloise blue. The touches of grape in the shadows and the lizard-green head help to make this parrot intensely rich without it screaming. Even the blacks are simply the deepest grey blues to be found. This bird is sheer elegance and would be at home in the rarest of antique rooms.

A dramatically different approach to birds can be found in the flat bright

Detail of birds from the *Gilbert White Memorial Window of St Francis* by Gascoyne & Hinks, English, 1920; Selborne Church, Hampshire, England.

Needlepoint in progress, *Peacock* by Kaffe Fassett, worked in tent stitch with wool yarns on 10-mesh canvas, 1990.

I chose Casteels' painting to demonstrate how one could approach the transforming of an artist's peacock into embroidery. You can see clearly how I begin by drawing the design on to the canvas with waterproof ink (left), and then go on to fill in the details while closely observing the painting. I have used about eight blues, ten golds and coppers, and pinks as well as browns and greens.

The fruit label peacock tail (right) is a more graphic study. This rendition concentrates on the contrasting colour details in each 'eye' on the feathers and on how they become deliciously smaller in scale as they get nearer to the body. You will often find that a cheap advertisement can supply you with a good basic layout which can be embellished with extra colour to make it as complex as any painting.

The Japanese plate (right) is a good example of a cool, blue and white design treatment, but with the unusual addition of pastel flowers and leaves. The fact that the design is mostly monotone serves to give the areas of high colour an extra vitality. This is an interesting colour balance to experiment with when designing.

For the more flamboyant amongst us the Chinese robe (right) supplies a

colours depicted in the *Gilbert White Memorial Window* (page 93). The window is such a moody study, containing many bird forms depicted in graphic linear detail. The black outline of the window leading is used to powerful effect. By keeping the majority of colours dark and tweedy in feeling, the black lines in the drawing, and those of the lead, work well in the scheme. The deep gold canary shines out of the stylish gloom.

This range of peacocks (right) demonstrates what I have set out to illustrate in this book. Different mediums bring out the staggering variety of approaches inherent in many subjects. From a common fruit label, by way of Oriental embroidery and porcelain, to fine European painting, we see how varied the results are.

Facing page

Detail of the peacock in the landscape painting *Peacock and Rabbits in a Landscape* by Pieter Casteels (1684–1749), oil on canvas.

Blue and white peacocks set in blue and white foliage with coloured flowers on a white ground, from a porcelain plate, Japanese, 19th century.

Detail of silk phoenix robe of Empress Dowager Tz'u-Hsi, Chinese, 19th century; Metropolitan Museum of Art, New York.

Detail of *Vandalia Brand* orange crate label, anonymous, offset colour lithograph, American, 20th century; The Fine Arts Museums of San Francisco.

burst of brilliant feathers in shades of turquoise, pink and gold all sitting in a bed of lavender. If you want something to 'read' a long way off a sunburst structure of lines radiating out from the centre is highly effective.

Having never seen an elephant in its natural setting, I always associate them with circuses and parades. An elephant painted, robed in fringed blankets and carrying a brightly coloured howdah is a child's vision of this huge, slow-moving creature. The ceramic menagerie (top right) is a reminder of this childhood vision. Stitched on to a cushion or chair cover or a carpet, this charming elephant would be very striking with its pink and blue drape, and the many animals and birds, all set on a banana-yellow ground.

The Mughal painting (left) shows lusciously how elephants appear in the wild. The steel grey of the elephants' bodies glows against the forest green and moss tones of the landscape. Those magenta highlights on stone outcroppings are wonderfully flame-like and the rich oranges and golds of the hunters' garments add an intensity to the painting. It is interesting to note that these brighter garment colours are not brash or obvious in any way because the oranges, golds and magentas have browny shadows that soften their impact. The range of green tones is quite extensive – mosses through to clear jades and high pea green, all on that dead-green base.

From a panel on a chest of drawers, the inlaid marble elephant (centre

Elephants in Battle, gouache, Mughal, circa 1770; India Office Library, London.

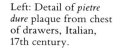

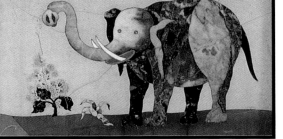

Left: *Group of Polito's Menagerie* by Obadiah Sherratt, ceramic, circa 1830.

Left: Detail of *pietre dure* plaque from chest of drawers, Italian, 17th century.

Below: Carved ivory elephant encrusted with semi-precious stones and mother-of-pearl flowers, Japanese, circa 1860.

right) has an endearingly witty expression. A frieze of wild animals like this elephant, all made in paper collage, would make a wonderful decoration for a child's room.

The ivory elephant (page 97), decked out in his jewelled finery, is quite a fantasy to behold. The grid of gems with rich tassels is a lovely detail, but the blanket of flowers and leaves in mother-of-pearl is truly outstanding. This all over mass of blossoms would make a gorgeous background for a simpler subject. If you do attempt to recreate these shell flowers, it is important to use all of the subtle lavenders, ochres and bluey silvers that you see in order to capture the richness of tone as well as scale – even the green leaves have their differing hues.

Here are some quite realistic animals (below and facing page) from the decorative arts. The porcelain tray has some wonderful detailed animals to design from. The kindly-faced camel, the red-eyed golden lion and the chestnut horse, are just a few of the cast that would make good models.

Porcelain tray with wild animals from Sèvres Tea Service, 1814; V&A Museum, London.

The soft landscape with tender pinky-lavender clouds could be a very valuable backdrop to a needlepoint. Can't you just picture stitching those mauvey, grey greens amongst the trees on the left of the picture? And that spotlit waterhole with the bright grass clump and silhouetted thistle plant would translate stunningly in wool or silk. Looking deeper into this *tour de force* of glazed porcelain, one's eye alights on the beautiful pastel fruits on the back of a faded zebra: another good detail to place in your own composition.

The foxes and grapes (right) is a panel from a screen containing many other animals and flowers. This panel demonstrates why I am always so delighted to see and feel autumn roll around each year. Fruit ripens on the vine and the all-prevailing green of summer is magically enriched to golds, reds and tawny browns. The last roses of the season appear so tender and blushing pink against these ochres tinged with scarlets.

Add to this mellow scene two coppery, cream-throated foxes and you have a winning colour scheme indeed. The washy sky ranging from deep cornflower to palest chalky grey blue has just enough tones to keep the whole work alive. The strong woody vines twist up the frame to contain the scene, then become art nouveau scrolls using the background colour with pink highlights. There is a good simplified tree mass in the background as well.

Monkeys . . . the very word conjures up agile cheeky brightness. The mon-

Screen panel depicting a fable by Aesop, Savonnerie, mid-18th century; Mobilier National, Paris.

key in the Frans Snyders painting (left) has a silky texture and lovely shades of buff on his back. The dark articulated face and feet should be good needle-point challenges.

I did my own watercolour (right) of this mother and child dusky leaf monkey, because I could not locate a painting showing their mask-like faces.

Bold contrasts in animals always give them a definition that makes them easier to portray than subtler colouring (see page 103). How wonderfully round those trailing-away lines make the zebra!

Perhaps we can learn something here about patterns on garments. Certainly this animal's extraordinary coat has often been used in fashion, but I do not recall ever seeing the stripes used with this gorgeous border of bright flowers which glow so colourfully against the cold black and white.

The washy sand background, turning to a soft flesh-tone blush around the body, is a beautiful contrasting setting for the sharpness of the zebra. Note that the only realistic shadowing on the animal is around the mouth, nose and ears, and the dark stripe running from the end of the mane down through the tail.

The flower colours are particularly alive and rich without being hard – lavender blue, mellow gold and sandy pink, with punctuations of hot, orange red on an eau-de-Nil-green vine. All of these flower colours sit comfortably on the sandstone backing, especially the chalky white with the blushes of dull pink shadows.

Detail of Still Life with a Red Deer by Frans Snyders (1579-1657), oil on canvas; Musée des Beaux-Arts, Marseilles.

Dusky Leaf Monkeys by Kaffe Fassett, watercolour, 1990.

The first thing that strikes one about the fifteenth-century French painting of the ark (page 102) is the beautiful aqua-coloured sea lapping about the charming little houseboat. Then the animals, with decidedly funny expressions, walking about the already crowded island come slowly into focus. On closer inspection we see the horrors of drowned corpses, some being savaged by crows, and elegant little house tops that have been swamped by the deluge. The whole teeming scene is painted in the most

Facing page: *Leaving the Ark* from *Bedford Book of Hours*, French, circa 1423; British Library, London.

harmonious cool pinks, singing blues and jade greens, with a delicate use of gold. Fiery scarlet and royal blue are reserved for the island people.

The animals are depicted in an almost comic strip form – exaggerated shapes with faces full of character. The decorative elements, like the white sheep walking with a black one between them, are quite amusing. The child-like proportions of the subjects and their crisp outlines have a charm that could be used well in your own designs.

It always amazes me how fluid a very stylized rendering of waves can appear. Here we have rows of diagonal stripes in shades of pale turquoise with regulated rows of dusty-mauve foam that actually gives the effect of water. Those people are drowning in it quite convincingly!

Above: *A Zebra* by Ustad Mansur, Mughal miniature, circa 1621; V&A Museum, London.

The older I get, the more I value my childhood impressions. Most of us as children had experience of pets and as a result have an intense perception of their special qualities. I mention this because later in life we seem to concentrate our awe on more exotic wild animals, forgetting the extreme charm of domestic animals.

Some time ago, when I wanted to create a tapestry on a farm theme, I combed the book shops of America and England for inspiring sources. It amazed me to find volumes on the wild beasts but nothing to speak of on the common hen, pig, cow or goose. Not surprisingly, however, the beloved household cat was well-served!

This oversight led me to produce a diary on farm animals (1991) and, of course, to present you with, I hope, a useful selection in this chapter.

The great beauty of domestic birds has always moved me and it is delightful to find that Italian artists of the thirteenth century felt the same. This witty, lively mosaic (left) depicts roosters, ducks, guinea fowl and other birds with a strong, bold hand. The colour is elegantly tweedy, incorporating tones that have graced many of the geometric patterns in my knitting.

I am full of admiration for these ancient artists' ability to describe so much character in a few crude chunks of glazed clay. The best thing about this source for non-drawers is that the very simple shapes of the birds can be so easily copied on to paper and then traced on to needlepoint canvas.

Domestic Animals

CHAPTER 5

Birds Entering the Ark, mosaic, Italian, 13th century; San Marco, Venice.

One of the first things one notices about roosters is how flamboyant and glamorous they are compared to the humble hens. Great tail feathers quiver as they strut, and artists from every corner of the world have used these proud birds as grand subjects.

The boldness of black and white figures prominently in the rooster sources (right) I have chosen for you. This will surprise those people whom I have advised to be wary of the colour white in designs. I have noticed that white is one repeated discrepancy in many would-be designers' attempts to use colour for the first

Rooster Cushion by Kaffe Fassett, needlepoint kit worked in tent stitch with wool yarns on 10-mesh canvas, 1988.

time. It is so glaringly strong that it knocks more gentle colourings into silhouettes. But there is no colour that cannot be used well and the refreshing contrast of black and white is an exciting element throughout the natural world. Black and white skunks, cats, zebras and butterflies cut quite a dash in their various habitats, and these smart looking birds are no exception.

It is interesting to speculate how black, white and scarlet seems to be a fashion perennial. Could it have started with the poultry world? Seeing the sharp patterns of two-colour feathers is exciting in a jazzy sort of way, but Millner's white cockerel silhouetted by the black hen has a creamy elegance of form.

Lovely soft tones of duck-egg blue, ochre and rust contrast beautifully with black and white on the Japanese porcelain cockerel. Its arched neck echoes the graceful shape of the tail feathers.

The vibrance of flowing feathers in d'Hondecoeter's seventeenth-century painting would be exciting to stitch in needlepoint. There is lots of contrast delineating each feather in the tail and the wing. And doesn't the luminous-blue sky light up the orange and ochre plumage and reflect into that tail wonderfully!

If you are looking for a more pared-down image to design from, the Indian rooster gouache has a spiky clarity in its plumage. Those tobacco golds and husky rusts are a brilliant foil for the steely shades of black on the tail and body.

You can see how the type of roosters pictured here inspired my *Rooster Cushion* (above). Always remember to pay as much attention to the background of your design as to the main

Facing page

Rooster gouache, Indian, mid-19th century; India Office Library, London.

Cock and Hen by Melchoir d'Hondecoeter (1636-1695) studio, oil on canvas.

Detail of chickens and goat from *Feeding the Chickens* by William Millner (1849-1895), oil on canvas.

Detail from *Poultry and a Peacock by a Cottage* by Eugen Frank, oil on canvas, 19th century.

Detail of *Cockerels in Landscape* by W.J. Shayer (1811-1885), oil on canvas.

Arita porcelain of multi-coloured cockerel, Japanese, circa 1688-1703.

Japanese Rooster and Hen by Kaffe Fassett and David Forrest, needlepoint kit worked in tent stitch with wool yarns on 10-mesh canvas, 1990.

subject. I rarely have a solid colour background in my needlepoint and for this rooster design I used the ochres of the wattle fence to set off effectively the black and white feathers.

When making a cushion cover like this one it is wise to add an extra border around your subject so that pertinent details do not get lost in the bulge of the cushion. I speak from experience here: I work designs right up to the edges of my canvas.

The densely detailed eighteenth-century painting by Itō Jakuchü (facing page) is a gift to a needlepoin-ter, as you can see from the embroidery (above) that it inspired. Layers of different coloured and patterned feathers have been depicted in a flat style that makes it easy to reproduce.

The number of colours in the original version had to be reduced so that it could be made into a kit, but you could work from this original source and use unlimited shades of browns, camels, reds and greens. A flat Japanese brocade pattern was chosen for the background but you could retain the flowers here or better still place the birds in a cabbage patch! A

Detail of *Rooster, Hen and Hydrangeas* by Itö Jakuchü (1716–1800), hanging scroll, colour on silk; Shin'enkan Collection, Los Angeles County Museum of Art.

Bulldog by Kaffe Fassett and Jill Gordon, needlepoint kit worked in tent stitch with wool yarns on 10-mesh canvas, 1990.

Printed fabric with ceramic dog, called *Staffordshire Dogs*, designed by Philip Jacobs for Ramm, Son & Crocker, 1989.

more structured setting, which would keep the whole picture a symphony of browns and greys, would be *The Farmyard* by Karl Uchermann on page 128.

Another idea for this Japanese source would be to centre the design around the whole rooster in all of his puffed up glory who, along with his partner, would make a handsome central focus for a needlepoint screen. They could be placed in an extensive garden scene with other animals added – like the mosaic cat on page 115.

You will notice at a glance that most of the dogs pictured here (this page and facing page) have strong brown, or black, and white markings. This is because I feel that these distinct

patterns are the easiest to reproduce in needlepoint stitches.

The stylized Staffordshire dogs on Philip Jacob's printed fabric (above right) could even be worked as knitted motifs. Having seen them in so many British homes and antique shops, I have always thought these ceramic dogs most amusing. Philip Jacobs designed them into a witty fabric with scrolls and roses, which would make a good theatrical setting for any of the more realistic dogs in this chapter.

The two Stubbs oils (on the facing page) have brilliantly painted dogs which are so carefully placed – posing for needlepoint designs you might say. Both paintings have wonderful greeny-brown backgrounds that set off the luminous coats.

Cut with bold patches of ebony, the great fluffy whiteness of the dog in Stubbs' *Fino and Tiny* is a treat. The warm tones in the white areas of his coat could be captured very realistically by using two or three colours of crewel threads together to make the subtle transitions. Shading smoothly

Facing page

Brown and White Norfolk or Water Spaniel by George Stubbs, oil on panel, 1778; Paul Mellon Collection, Upperville, Virginia.

The 7th Duke of Beaufort's Dogs, Lion and Dash by Sir Edwin Landseer, oil, circa 1840; Duke of Beaufort, Badminton.

Two Bulldogs by G. Jones, oil on panel of two dogs against a black background, 1872.

Greyhound by Philip Reinagle (1749-1833), oil on canvas depicting a black and white greyhound and a hare against a landscape.

Spaniels Galore by John Emms (1843-1912), oil on canvas depicting eight brown and white spaniels on stone steps.

Detail of *Fino and Tiny* by George Stubbs, oil on canvas, 1791; The Royal Collection, London.

from moss green to deep Van Dyke brown in the landscape behind him could be achieved in the same way.

The tones in the shadow areas of Stubbs' Water Spaniel's curly cream coat (page 110) would be a joy to try to capture in tent stitch. If you do try it, make the dog large enough so that you can get in all of the detail, or work him on a fine mesh needlepoint canvas.

The huge old St Bernard by Landseer (page 110) is a good subject, too, with his great sad eyes and his silky camel and cream coloured fur. Placing him against a scarlet blanket is a wonderful dramatic device.

Repeating images are always fascinating, and Emms' *Spaniels Galore* (page 110) is no exception! Their rusty ears tone well with the old bricks.

The lean body of Philip Reinagle's *Greyhound* (page 110) has a stunning silhouette, the markings are sharp and emphasize the line down the back into that superbly curved tail.

But for outrageous character it was the bulldog in G. Jones' painting that caught my assistant Jill Gordon's, and my, attention. Jill stitched him beautifully into a needlepoint cushion kit (page 111). The addition of plaids in two different scales and colourings makes a striking backdrop for this mutt with his expressive eyes, great floppy tongue and big gentle paws.

Any of the bejewelled, gussied-up dogs in Tiberio di Tito's painting on pages 112 and 113 would make delightful subjects, either separately or in groups. The red ribbon earrings and ruffles underline their pampered little faces. Their bored keeper looks rather dog-like himself, grown weary with it all.

By now you will see that I have a passion for mosaics. This third-century Roman mosaic of a cat and a duck (right) has the feeling of a beaded surface. You cannot help but marvel at the quality of fur achieved on the cat and the featheriness of the ducks. There is such life and vigour in the 'drawing' of these animals and such a lovely sense of light created by the simplest means.

You can usually learn a lot by copying the very basic way these early artists achieved the illusion of living creatures. It is all done with little squares of glass or stone that could well be represented by needlepoint tent stitches. Very subdued, rather tweedy, tones have been used here, but you could enrich the design for embroidery by adding deep greens and brighter rust tones to the ducks.

Why do we love cats so much! If we don't hate them we usually have a fascination for these mysterious creatures. Their innate confidence and ability to pose in the most gorgeous setting they can find are part of the cat's attraction. Whenever I lay a newly finished needlepoint or knitted garment on the floor to study, a cat invariably strolls up to place itself in the middle of the work, looking ravishing.

The eighteenth-century Chinese version of kittens in a garden (page 116) emphasizes the playfulness they are famous for. A soft shadow around each

Cat Devouring a Partridge and a Mallard, mosaic, Roman, 3rd century; National Museum, Naples.

Kittens at Play by Leon Huber, oil on canvas, 19th century.

animal and blurred markings depict their fluffiness wonderfully.

One of my all-time favourite cat paintings is the daft cat in a hatbox (facing page). It displays such an attention to detail, particularly in the bashed-up box and in the beautiful ochre shades of the floor and wall. Painted by a Dutch diamond cutter, the work has the elegant restraint I associate with Holland. To top it off there is such a lovely humour in the placement of the subject.

Facing page

Detail from a scroll after Hsüan Tsung (reigned 1389-1435), colours on silk, Chinese, 18th century; Metropolitan Museum of Art, New York.

Cat with Fish, painting by anonymous artist, Indian (Kalighat), 19th century; V&A Museum, London.

A cat sitting in an archway, marquetry by Fra' Raffaele da Brescia, Italian, early 16th century; Abbey of Monte Oliveto Maggiore Abbazia, Italy.

Strange Contents by Sal Meyer (1877-1965), oil on canvas, 1909; Stedelijk Museum, Amsterdam.

As for the marquetry cat (facing page) – hasn't she found her medium! The grain of the cut wood pieces perfectly describes her tortoise-shell fur. The curved upright back and direct stare make this an excellent design source. I love the classical arched setting and distant landscape.

The Indian painting of a cat (facing page) is a masterstroke of boldness. Huge black markings on buttercup yellow with orange shadows delineate the form to a tee. The fish may have the appearance of being glued on, but no matter: this confident approach should encourage us to draw quickly what we feel.

Leon Huber's kitsch little kittens (above), with their glass marble eyes and fluffy coats, are a bit over cute, but

117

Pansy the Cow by Kaffe Fassett, needlepoint kit worked in tent stitch with wool yarns on 10-mesh canvas, 1988.

I have included them as a design source for you because of the setting of rich red golds and lavenders that attracted my eye.

I could gaze for hours at black and white cows with their great rectangles of abstract pattern. Here is the boldest design in the animal kingdom – massive patches of black on creamy white. The vision of a field of cows in their never ending variety is astounding. Painting them would be a great pleasure, and I intend to do that when I start painting seriously again.

My *Pansy the Cow* needlepoint cushion (above left) was worked from a Rory Mitchell photograph. The mosaic border with pansy tiles was added to recall the feeling of old dairy shops. It is interesting how three-dimensional she looks with the use of only seven colours.

Artists of many cultures have been attracted to this subject. The Dutch here provide us with two extremes – a delightful Delft fantasy dripping in flowers and red polka dots on a colourful base (above right) and a beautifully simple rendition in watercolour and gouache by Erno Tromp (facing page). All of the shadow areas in Tromp's Friesian cow have been beautifully abstracted and articulated so that they are perfect for the decorative artist to work from.

For even simpler examples the Indian and Egyptian cows (facing page) are depicted in just black and white with little shading. The success of this pared-down rendering depends on getting that familiar silhouette and bold markings to read 'cow'.

The Egyptian artist made the organic shapes of black into a jolly de-

Tin-glazed earthenware cow, Dutch (Delft), 18th century; The Metropolitan Museum of Art, New York.

sign of diamonds and dots with a few deft strokes of a brush. The ochre, rust and teal blue make a superb ground to put the bull on. Because it is a strong clear statement, yet has a soft 'liveable with' palette, this bull could be worked into a handsome needlepoint. It would also be a wonderfully simple source to knit from.

The Cornell Farm by Edward Hicks (following pages) reminds one of what a wealth of colours cows come in. The duns, buffs, rusts and ochres make us even more aware of the extraordinary shape of the beast. The body seems to hang from an amazing structure like a great laundry hamper. These soft colours are so beautiful as a group.

There are many ways to use Hicks' crowded painting. The deliciously dappled cows in so many shades could provide lots of interpretations. The row of trees on the green lawn could be a good background for many of the subjects in this book, as could the simple barns.

Always on the lookout for interesting skies, I could be tempted to use this very delicate, blushing sky for a subtle touch to a design. For a wildly chromatic sky the Indian miniature (right) is nothing to sneeze at! The great rolling red clouds and rich gold horizon could furnish the appropriate drama for a strong subject.

One can see why horses are so appealing to young girls – they have powerful bodies that can carry people about or haul great loads yet at the same time have elegant sensitive heads. My own early encounters with

Cattle Breeds I, Black and White Dutch Friesian Cow by Erno Tromp, watercolour and gouache on paper, 1984.

Scene from the Bagavatta Purana, Indian miniature, 18th century; New Delhi Museum.

Apis the Sacred Bull, painting in the tomb of Sunnutem at Thebes, Egyptian, 1292 BC.

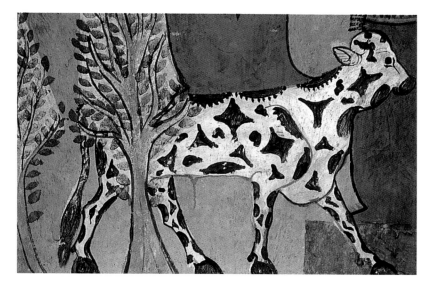

Balotade (classical equestrianism) by unknown artist, oil, 1691-1694; Rosenborg Castle, Copenhagen.

Top above: Micromosaic panel of a bull, 7.6cm (3in) wide, Italian, 19th century.

Above: *Portrait of the Horse, Amber Head*, gouache on paper, Mughal, 17th century; British Museum, London.

Previous page: *The Cornell Farm* by Edward Hicks, oil on canvas, 1848; National Gallery of Art, Washington.

Horses by Utagawa Hiroshige II (1826-1869), colour woodcut from *A New Publication*, circa 1847-1848; The Fine Arts Museums of San Francisco.

horses helped me develop a sense of respect for them, having been thrown and having watched others have difficulties at my father's riding stables.

Looking at these horse paintings (this page and facing page) you cannot help being struck by the nervous energy held within these handsome beasts. The Japanese study of horses by Utagawa Hiroshige II (facing page) captures wonderfully the spirited postures they assume.

Personally, I am drawn to the massive work horses. Their great nobby joints and powerful necks make good models to draw from. You will find many good examples in nineteenth-century landscape paintings.

For its pure aesthetic elegance of line the seventeenth-century Mughal painting (left below) is a poetic study. The soft sage green perfectly shows off the luminous white and cinnamon stallion.

Because I am a knitter, people often think that I am wildly interested in sheep. Actually, I find them a bit monotone for my taste, but the painting by Charles Jones (page 124) portrays the Welsh sheep with such a richness in the evening light that they become intricate landscapes. Every tuft and fold of fur and face is so lovingly painted. Those of you who are

Detail of *Welsh Black-faced Sheep* by Charles Jones (1836–1892), oil on canvas.

into sheep could work a magnificent needlepoint from this source. It is populated with so many shades of amber, ivory, ochre, pale blue and cream, not to mention the deep browns and blue blacks of the heads. There are also luscious golden undertones as well as deep moss greens in the grass.

The fourteenth-century Italian painting by Bartolo di Fredi (facing page) has an impressively intricate flock of sheep filling the bottom of the picture. All these lined-up heads and backs, and the dangling confusion of dark legs, are captivating.

I have always been drawn to objects in unison; there is something about a repeated shape which underlines the richness of variety that we experience in all natural things. It is good that Bartolo di Fredi's sheep are all different colours so their wavy coats are separated. The rest of the painting is packed with enticing details – camels, rich robes and a beautiful hill town of pink and pistachio houses.

Goats are real characters with their beards, extraordinary horns and spotted coats. The approaches of many different artists seen here tell of a wide

Abramo si divide da Lot by Bartolo di Fredi, fresco, 14th century; Duomo, San Gimignano, Italy.

interest in this farmyard rascal. The Meissen piece (facing page) has a tailor parading on a lovely black and white dappled goat. The tailor's primrose-yellow coat sprinkled with flowers is a good knitting idea.

For a realistically detailed mode, the oil by Edgar Hunt (facing page) displays lovely shades of smoky browns, honeys and creams. Being very partial to green eyes I find his wondrous.

The William Hunt watercolour (facing page) shows a grubby chap with turned-down horns, while the *Shawl Goat* (right) is a sleek-coated creature with elegantly turned-up horns and a strong stance.

For a much more stylized goat the bold black and white one in the fifteenth-century Indian miniature (facing page) makes a sharp impression against the overlapping greenery. Those primitive leaves are wonderfully effective in a few shades. You could certainly expand on the number of colours and use this abstracted jungle of foliage as a background for many types of subject.

The Farmyard by Karl Uchermann (page 128) has one of my favourite settings. A symphony of weathered-wood tones – from deep Van Dyke browns through to chestnut reds to silvery greys – inhabit this scene. The

dusty courtyard is a warm neutral tone that is all but indistinguishable from the bottom of the wood surfaces. In all this muted world sits a glowing pig and some splendid fowl.

The brushwork is clear enough on the pig to encourage some good rich colour changes when one is stitching from the piggy-flesh tones with dusty-copper shadows. There is a lovely warm, slightly world-weary, expression on the pig's face. (Do I see Boris Becker's thick blond eyelashes?) The pig has a bemused smile, neat little feet and a delicious curl in his tail.

Top above: Detail of *The Goatherd* by Julius Paul Junghans (1876-1953), oil on canvas.

Above: *Shawl Goat*, gouache, Indian, 18th century; India Office Library, London.

Right: Detail of *The Farmyard* by Karl K. Uchermann (1855–1940), oil on canvas.

Below: *Profile of a Hare* by Takeuchi Seiho, colour woodcut, circa 1915–1920; The Fine Arts Museums of San Francisco.

The child's expression, as he is held by his big sister, is slightly apprehensive. The rooster in the farmyard is deftly painted in an extensive range of colours. The blacks have highlights of lavender blue, and the reds go from a tomato cockscomb, through ochrey rusts, to faded burgundy back feathers. That well-painted white hen is thoughtfully placed to show off the rooster's jaunty black tail feathers.

Trying to achieve the glow of those wooden barns in tent stitch would be a real test in handling colour. Within that dark to light range are to be found shots of red, gold, and platinum. These raw colours are so assimilated into the soft tones that they give a

Above: *The Rabbits' Feast* by Henry Garland (flourished 1840–1890), oil on canvas.

Right: Needlepoint kit in progress, *Rabbits* by Kaffe Fassett and David Forrest, worked in tent stitch with wool yarns on 10-mesh canvas, 1990.

mysterious life to a subtle dusty scene that emerges only after some observation. I like to do this in my knitting and needlepoint as often as possible – imbue a subtle colour scheme with hidden 'sparks' of colours. Lavender is a great 'spark' colour with greys, for example.

There is a Victorian sweetness that comes close to being over cute in Garland's painting (above). But the Victorians with all their sentiment were keen observers of life. These watery eyes and luxurious fur coats are cast in a beautiful glowing light that works well as a needlepoint (right).

This needlepoint was begun to show just one of the many ways to approach

129

Egyptian Ducks by Kaffe Fassett, watercolour, 1975.

the subject, which was to select the two central rabbits and feature the glorious cabbage leaf and blue and white plate.

The small embroidered fragment of the rabbits hit such a chord with all who saw it that it has now been de-

veloped into a kit (see page 191 for kit information). There is quite a bold strength in the painting source for all its detail. The straw is simplified enough to be easy to capture in needlepoint. These chaps would also look at home in a vegetable garden setting or even under a rose bush.

Many people have a passion for ducks which I certainly share. The expensive handpainted decoys in shops and galleries and the brilliant knitting patterns with ducks by designer Susan Duckworth spring to my mind.

Geese, on the other hand, are not so universally depicted which, given their statuesque figures, is a mystery to me. Simple snowy-white geese are

Facing page

Detail of two ducks from *Ducks on the Shore* by Archibald Thorburn (1860-1935), oil on canvas of ducks in a landscape.

Detail of a black swan with cygnets from *Black Swans in a Winter Landscape* by G. West, oil on canvas, 19th century.

Barnacle Goose, hand-coloured aquatint by R.H. Havell from Audubon's *Birds of America* (1827-38); British Museum (Natural History), London.

Geese from *To Pastures New* by Sir James Guthrie (1859-1930), oil on canvas; Aberdeen Art Gallery and Museums, Scotland.

Common Sheldrake by Prideaux John Selby from Selby's *Waterbirds* (1818-34), hand-coloured engraving; Linnean Society, London.

Geese and Poultry Feeding by Edgar Hunt (1876-1953), oil on canvas of a grey goose and two grey and white geese eating vegetables in a farmyard.

gorgeous enough but the addition of greys, browns and black makes them startlingly exciting to work into designs.

The sharpest specimen here (page 130) is the Common Sheldrake with his brilliant golden ochre band of feathers, lacquered beak and ebony head.

The pinky-orange feet and beaks provide a warm note to Edgar Hunt's geese (page 130) with their cool steel greys on white. But, for an action-filled stance, Havell's *Barnacle Goose* (page 130) is marvellously articulated. You could use his pose for whichever colouring you prefer.

For pure drama the *Black Swans* by West (page 130), against the frozen backdrop, take the prize. The lipstick-red beak and subtle shades of black emphasize the swan's impossibly beautiful neck. The pinks and frosty corn tones in the grasses create a richly-toned setting.

The Thorburn ducks (page 130) are stunning because of the tone-on-tone quality of all those toasty shades. The lavender blues work so well as a cool element in the otherwise warm colour scheme. It is amazing how many shades are used here – hot tobaccos, rich chestnuts and soft minky tones. How luminous the water appears in its mysterious neutral shade.

James Guthrie's painting of a flock of big sunny geese (page 130) takes me straight back to my childhood. My mother kept lemons in a bowl that was fashioned to resemble a ring of geese. I loved that funny thing with a passion and did many paintings of it.

My sketch of ducks (page 131) is from an outstanding Egyptian painting in the Brooklyn Museum, New York. The overlapping heads fascinated me, and I used them in a printed fabric for a New York fashion house.

The monumental elegance of the turkey always amazes me. When you analyse the elements of this great bird there is not much to recommend it – a lumpy red neck, small eyes, brown feathers and a fat body. Yet, when we behold the whole bird, it has an impressive grandness. The painter who created this gouache (facing page) obviously thought so and placed his subject beautifully on a cool green field studded with four blooming plants.

Each feather of the turkey is so simple, so sharply delineated. The shading from pale beige to dusty pink in the wing creates a wonderful effect, just vaguely broken with the palest of gunmetal greys. Being very attracted to decadence, I quite like the crumbled quality of this early seventeenth-century painting.

Turkey, Mughal School, gouache on paper, early 17th century; Fitzwilliam Museum, Cambridge, England.

133

tely I have had a love affair with cabbages – this has led me into a whole leafy world. Painting or stitching leaves seems to sharpen one's perception of the many varieties of foliage to be seen, even in the heart of cities. Living within walking distance of London's Hampstead Heath I have at my disposal a wonderful sprawl of wild hills covered with an astounding array of foliage. Delicate grasses and wild flowers cavort with massive chestnuts and gunnera plants. What a joy it is to find such a place in one of the world's largest cities. As I run or swim in the outdoor pond on the Heath, I am constantly dazzled by the changing beauty of willows, elms, oaks and all the other species that abound in this well-loved park on London's doorstep.

The little landscape in Desportes' *Indian Hunter* tapestry cartoon (left) reminds me of the Heath's lush swimming pond. The painting displays such a wonderful variety of foliage dotted with exotic fruits, not to mention a menagerie of birds and creatures of the sea. The big bluish spade-shaped leaves in the foreground make perfect needlepoint design sources because they are excitingly lit with strong shadows and silvery highlights. For wild elongated leaves, the variegated plants in the right-hand corner are very Rousseau-like and again clearly defined against the darker bush. Their ribbon stripes help them to 'read' as leaves in a tapestry.

Just a few of the extraordinarily vast range of decorative trees that

The Indian Hunter by Alexandre François Desportes (1661-1743), cartoon for the tapestry *Les Nouvelles Indes*, oil on canvas; Musée des Beaux-Arts, Marseilles.

CHAPTER 6

designers have to draw on are given here (on the facing page).

Particularly engaging are the formalized interpretations of trees which are found in the early decorative arts. The scale of the crown and trunk are drastically reduced while the individual leaves are greatly enlarged. The tree on the sixteenth-century English cushion cover is a good example of this type of design. The fruits and leaves in their enormous childlike detail are beautifully embroidered against the theatrical black ground.

Other artists stylize organic shapes into tight, geometric structures like the red-barked forest in the painting by Tamas Galambos and the delightful Roman mosaic tree. The mirror image of the mosaic tree flanked by spotted animals would translate well into knitting. I have already used spotted animals like these two protectors in my *Heraldic Dog Sweater* (page 82).

The world of 'primitive' arts, so full of expressive subjects, should give us all confidence to have a go at drawing and stitching whether we have had formal training or not. These unaffected statements are so lively yet at the same time so simple that they cannot fail to touch all who behold them.

Carpets and embroideries make use of repeating tree motifs to great effect, as seen here in the Baktiari carpet. Equally good motifs can be found in Greek and Turkish embroideries.

Often in Indian and Persian miniatures each leaf of a tree is painted with great precision, thus producing plants in strangely sharp focus. Notice how the leaves on the Mughal miniature have as strong a sculptural quality as the jewelled Fabergé tree, where each leaf is a delicately carved jade stone.

Probably the biggest influence on my own work comes from the world of old tapestries with their rich, warm colours. From the stylized details of the medieval Unicorn tapestries to the more realistic effects of later weavings, the shapes are wonderfully abstracted making them very accessible for use as design elements. With just three shades of green – the bright highlight in the foreground, the medium tone and the dark shadow – a complex foliage with great depth and energy can be created.

There are an endless number of gorgeous examples of trees and foliage to be found in the decorative and fine arts and these pages are only meant to point you towards the riches you can find in

Facing page

Triangular-shaped tree detail from *La Dame à la Licorne*, woven tapestry, French, 15th century; Musée Cluny, Paris.

Detail of *Alamgir Deer Hunting*, Mughal miniature, 1675; Philadelphia Free Library, Philadelphia, USA.

Detail of stylized red trees from *The Legend of the White Deer* by Tamas Galambos, oil on canvas, 20th century.

Orange Tree Egg by Fabergé, jewels and precious metals, Russian, 19th century; Forbes Magazine, New York.

Fancie of the Flower, embroidered cushion cover, English, late 16th century; Hardwick Hall, Derbyshire.

Garden with Centaurs, Leopards and Peacocks, detail of mosaic in the Palozzo dei Normanni, 12th century; Palermo, Italy.

Study of Trees by Felix Vallotton, oil on canvas, 1911; Musée des Beaux Arts, Quimper, France.

Detail of *Orlando Furioso*, woven tapestry, Dutch, 17th century; Museo Poldi Pezzoli, Milan.

Repeating tree motifs alternating with other repeating motifs, Baktiari carpet, Persian, 1910.

Detail of 15th-century
tapestry which is
shown on the
preceding pages.

tent and tree patterns all sitting on that robustly ornate ground make the work vibrate with vitality. That pink on deeper pink brocade as a background pops up repeatedly in French Gobelin tapestries.

The glorious spiralling top of the tent and the curly pattern of the garments inspired my knitted *Fossil Jacket* (right). In the knitting the flat, even, two-toned tent pattern has been streaked with several tones and textures to give it added life. This does obscure the pattern a little so do try it more like the tapestry if you prefer the clarity of three colours. The tapestry version has a rather Matisse paper cutout feel about it. There could be an endless game of trying different colours on these knitted shapes. Some might like very dark colours in forest green, deep plum on black, or even a perky pastel rendition in cotton for summer.

The tapestry lends itself to several other design ideas. The red-outlined pelmet and flower border of the tent (left) are captivating. And there is a delicious little pattern of leaves on deep pink inside the tent.

The explosion of luminous-green poppy leaves in Kokei Kobayashi's scroll (page 142) takes one's breath away. What an elegant dance the veins perform, twisting this way and that. Knowing from experience how difficult it is to handle greens, I take my hat off to the artist for finding so many delicately differing shades of cool jade greens. Even the stems and buds are lovingly painted and add to the energy

museums and books. Another brilliant source of lucidly illustrated plantlife is Chinese handpainted wallpaper. Also, the lush island cultures such as Haiti and Bali often produce sumptuous paintings of overlapping trees with layer upon layer of flat patterns, built up into a magical forest.

When first glancing at this fifteenth-century tapestry (pages 138 and 139) I was not too impressed and felt it looked a little like a wrapping paper design. However, after studying it over several months and considering the period when it was made, I was more and more moved by its flamboyant life. The vigorous garment,

Fossil Jacket by Kaffe
Fassett, knitting kit,
wool yarns, 1990.

The Aged Mullah by Farrakh Beq, Mughal miniature, Shah Jehan period, 1630; V&A Museum, London.

fantasy of a tree with fresh, pointing leaves in a bizarre range of colours. All of the colours used are possible in the tree world, but somehow placing them so evenly throughout the painting makes it appear quite improbable, but delightful. The burnt reds, pinks, pale and deep yellows are beautifully at home on the ochre ground.

The della Robbia border tiles (pages 144 and 145) are a perfect example of the diversity of foliage available to us. The motifs on the tiles are so gloriously simplified without appearing in the least flat or two-dimensional. It is striking how all of these disparate leaf forms fit into the oval format so harmoniously.

The sixth-century mosaic (page 145) is notable for its leafy madness and the sixteenth-century tapestry (page 144) for its wonderful, monumental leaves. You will find similar thrilling all-foliage tapestries in the Rijksmuseum in Amsterdam.

For very stylized forms the ecclesiastical robe (page 144) really is inspired. This sort of design, if copied element by element, is very easy to make use of. That peachy terracotta melts so beautifully into the high chartreuse greens and sky blue of the flowers.

One day I was asked to do a tapestry for a fan who wanted to treat herself.

in this painting. You can feel it growing as you look at it!

After all the striking beauty of green come the carefully painted flowers – huge creamy blossoms with the palest of shadows and blood-red poppies bursting from their bud encasements. These poppies would be stunning on a large needlepoint wallhanging. Or a sensational high-backed chair would be much enhanced by the flowers and leaves stitched on to the back and more leaves on the seat.

The seventeenth-century Indian miniature (above) presents us with a joyful

Overleaf

Facing page: Poppies by Kokei Kobayashi (1881-1957), hanging scroll; Tokyo National Museum.

Woven chasuble with stylized leaves, flowers and other plant motifs, silk and gold, circa 1700; Pitti Palace, Florence.

Detail of border with pomegranates by Luca della Robbia (1400-circa 1482); S. Trinita, Florence.

Detail of border with white lilies by Luca della Robbia (1400-circa 1482), glazed maiolica; S. Trinita, Florence.

Verdure tapestry fragment of green leaves and three small angels, French, 16th century.

Mosaic from the Great Palace of the Emperors, Byzantine, probably 6th century AD; Mosaics Museum, Istanbul.

Detail of border with black olives by Luca della Robbia (1400-circa 1482); S. Trinita, Florence.

Detail of border with white flowers by Luca della Robbia (1400-circa 1482), glazed maiolica; S. Trinita, Florence.

Illuminated initial by Liberale da Verona, Italian, 15th century; Piccolomini Library, Duomo, Sienna.

Green Parrots by Kaffe Fassett, needlepoint worked in long stitch with wool yarns on 8-mesh canvas, 1988.

Lemon by Jacques le Moyne de Morgues (circa 1533–1588), watercolours and bodycolours, circa 1585; British Museum, London.

'What subject?' I asked. 'Well, I like green . . . and I have a parrot,' came the reply.

Into my head flashed a leafy tree with green parrots. She then sent me a glorious book called *Parrots of the World* as a reference and we were off! I grabbed every green parrot out of that book and rifled through my drawers of cuttings to find green leaf sources.

One day during my search a postcard arrived with the le Moyne de Morgues' sixteenth-century lemons on it and my heart stopped! What gorgeous crisp leaves and mellow lemons (left). My assistant, Elian, incorporated the lemons into the scheme before you could blink (above). Steve Lovi sug-

Detail of *Tiger Shoot*, gouache, Indian, circa 1825.

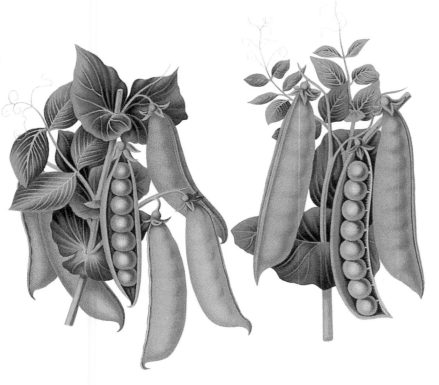

Above: *Peas* from *Album Benary*, lithograph, 1876; Royal Horticultural Society, London.

Right: Dish by Jacob Petit, porcelain, French, 1850; V&A Museum, London.

Below: *Cabbages* from *Album Benary*, lithograph, 1876; Royal Horticultural Society, London.

gested a soft green background, but fearing the leaves would be lost I went for the peachy sky fading to pale blue.

When I look at the Indian painting (page 147) I wish I had used a green background. How sumptuous those many shades look! In order to make this type of design work in needlepoint you have to decide on the background tone, then make each added green contrast enough to read. The dark bottle greens, pale jades and yellow greens work superbly on the rich grass tones.

Pearly peas in crisp green cases and voluptuous leafy cabbages – sounds like heaven to me! Ever since I did my first cabbage and cauliflower needlepoint cushion kits a couple of years ago, I have grown increasingly passionate about beautiful fruits and vegetables. The many shades of greens in melons and cabbages are stimulating enough to work from, but the deep mysteriously off-tones of the purple cabbage make it a magical experience.

The Greengrocer by Willem van Mieris (1662-1747), oil on panel; The Wallace Collection, London.

A *famille rose* tobacco-leaf porcelain plate, Chinese, 18th century.

Artichoke by Kaffe Fassett, needlepoint kit worked in tent stitch with wool yarns on 7-mesh canvas, 1990.

Globe Artichoke by Jacques le Moyne de Morgues (circa 1533-1588), watercolours and bodycolours, French, circa 1585; British Museum, London.

The cabbages lithograph from the *Album Benary* (page 148) is a gift to a needlepoint designer who is into a darker palette and wants a jaunty object for a chair, tapestry or cushion. Imagine it set among black grapes, maroon pansies and beetroots.

The vegetable world also has its more brilliant colour schemes. The nineteenth-century French porcelain dish (page 148) of shallots, radishes, asparagus and hot red pimentos, all in high colours, would instantly make a table into a party.

For a marvellously brazen use of colour and shapes the Chinese tobacco-leaf design (page 148) has long been one of my favourite plate decorations. The huge, expressively painted leaves with gaudy flowers are truly dramatic. Just imagine doing those leaves in duck-egg, cobalt and royal blue, along with primrose and shaded dusty pink! The designer was inspired! This design begs to be knitted or stitched into exciting designs.

Artichokes are impressive with their solid handsomeness. I lived near vast

Previous page: *Still Life* by Jan van Kessel (1626-1679), oil on copper; Galleria Doria, Rome.

fields of them in California. The huge arched, elegantly spiky leaves are so beautiful that I used to grow them for decoration in my garden. This study by le Moyne de Morgues (page 150), an artist I am more and more respectful of, sparked me off to design a cushion cover (page 151).

The powerful lavender and inky bottle-green shadow on this painting make it irresistibly real. I would like to do another version in finer tent stitch using the leaf and that small dark artichoke as well.

Somehow morning glories found their way into my needlepoint artichoke design as a border. The cool duck-egg background with warm terracotta edges seemed right. But dark burgundy or warm grey would give another atmosphere altogether. A sturdy round shape like this artichoke could figure well as a repeat pattern staggered with flowers' heads.

As a painter I am hugely impressed by the restrained control of the brushwork in Jan van Kessel's table of fruit (pages 152 and 153). Every hair on the animals, every leaf and petal and wicker on the baskets is so lovingly painted. It has that crammed surface that I employ in most of my still lifes. And the addition of leaves, luscious fruits and flowers to the handsome crocks and baskets makes this table dance for joy.

The shades in this painting are superb for a gentle colour scheme. The warm putty-coloured table and gunmetal wall set off the sage-green leaves and mellow sandstone yellows most

elegantly. Even the reds are soft veiled persimmon shades, and the blue and white whispers its gently faded presence. All the animals are brown black and creamy white, except for the red squirrel and the green parrot.

There are a hundred good design sources in this one painting, exquisitely drawn for the needlepointer. To name but a few, there are the grapes on the wall, the branch of cherries, the monkey against his magnificent basket of fruits, the broken bowl of raspberries, and those stunning bouquets of flowers.

One of the cautionary tales to be learnt here is the way the monkey's black face all but disappears into those dark plums. Moving a red apple to the right would give him more definition. Note the little hamster with his handsome contrast colours.

There is something intriguing about how simply and effectively Hodgkin has arranged disparate subjects on a plain, hinted-at flat surface (facing page). Gorgeous natural objects like these are difficult to pull oneself away from. How miraculous each and every item is to behold.

Peering at a humble bean, head of garlic or brussel sprout fills me with wonder, so I am grateful for painters like this one who paint with such loving precision in order to spotlight the specialness of everyday vegetables.

The autumn leaves of the *November* drawing are noteworthy – the golden leaf emerging out of apple green deepening into copper orange at the edges and the dark-green leaf with

Six drawings from *Twelve Months of the Year* by Eliot Hodgkin, tempera on board, 1950-1951.

Eliot Hodgkin April 1951

Eliot Hodgkin · June 1950

Eliot Hodgkin November 50

Eliot Hodgkin May 1951

Baskets of Fruit on the Steps of a Terrace by William Hammer, oil on canvas, 1852.

Embroidered chair decorated with grapes, worked by Countess Thott for the Manor House of Gaunø, wool and silk worked in *gros point* on needlepoint canvas, 1750; Danish Museum of Decorative Arts, Copenhagen.

husky maroon borders tinged with fire. Another special detail which stands out is the two stalks of asparagus. The satiny shimmer of lavender tints melt into luminous green from creamy white. They have the quality of being fashioned from glass. The pinky-green grapes in *October* also have a glassy look to them.

It is instructive to look at the range of yellows in all of these drawings. There is no raw lemon yellow, all of the 'yellows' are mellow golds and ochres, the brightest being the chrysanthemum in the corner of *October*. The reds also have such a rich-toned quality, the strawberry and tulip in *May* being the highest.

Looking at one source after another to use in various needlepoint projects, you will be excited to see how someone in the past has made a splendid piece using the same medium. Countess Thott's chair (facing page) is a fine *tour de force* from the Danish Museum of Decorative Arts in Copenhagen. The subtle range of colours and beautiful drawing and shading make this a work to aspire towards. The grapes and leaves are so carefully observed and interpreted.

William Hammer's *Baskets of Fruit* (above) is an equally tasteful arrangement of subtle tones. It is as if there is a mist making the autumn light as pearly as a London morning in September.

Still Life by Luca Forte, oil, 18th century.

Still Life by Tsuguji Foujita (1886–1968), oil on canvas. © ADAGP, Paris and DACS, London 1991.

A Still Life of Plums and Jam-making Utensils by Paul Gagneux, oil on canvas, late 19th century.

Hammer has used a device I like to use so much, which is to create a neutral-toned space that will make all those reds, greens, and soft yellows glow happily. There is nothing coming close to stark white and no inky black; yet, without using any hard contrast, areas of drama arise.

There is a smooth flow of colour in Luca Forte's study of grapes (top left) that is quite fascinating. It makes the apples, in particular, appear rather monumental, like great golden globes. If you want to capture the same mood in your work be careful not to create

Cup with Strawberries and Pears and Grasshopper Eating Wheat by Giovanna Garzoni (1600-1670), tempera on parchment; Palatine Gallery, Florence.

abrupt changes of tone which would produce hard, contrasting edges. The 'blushes' of colour on these apples are just that, softly moving from red through pink to gold with a satin highlight or two on each piece. Even the shadows on the lit-up floor have slightly blurred edges.

When looking at Gagneux's plums (facing page) aren't you astounded at the range of colour and infinite variety that exists in the same fruit? Yellows, pinks, peaches, lavenders, all emerge under a silvery-sage bloom – and all that against smouldering copper! The

English engineer, Jeremy Fry, once constructed a dining room lined entirely with sheets of copper with a leather floor. The effect created a warm pinky glow that made everyone feel euphoric.

Giovanna Garzoni uses an astounding variety of scales and colourings in her still life (above) of wild strawberries and pears.

Tsuguji Foujita's fruits (facing page) have a high, sunny quality. The painting is very loosely painted with a quick brush. Those spidery leaves give a craggy life to the composition.

Gascoyne Scarlet Apples (far left) and *Ribston Pippin Apples* (near left) by Rosanne Sanders, from *The English Apple*, watercolour, 1988.

Cabbage and Apple Carpet by Kaffe Fassett, needlepoint carpet kit worked in tent stitch with wool yarns on 8-mesh canvas, 1989.

Ever since I saw my first Cézanne still life, apples have attracted my attention. But finding good apple sources for my needlepoints has always been difficult. One day I stumbled across Rosanne Sanders' book *The English Apple* and knew it was manna from heaven. Every page glows with dazzlingly fresh and glowing apples (see above). I never knew there were so many varieties of apples in the whole world, let alone England!

The *Cabbage and Apple Carpet* (facing page) was designed as several squares sewn together so that embroiderers could have fun stitching with friends. Each person in the group can take a square to work on. Nothing would please me more than the revival of the old quilting bees. Working together as

a group encourages artistic growth, and we all need a pat on the back as we create something. It also gives that strong sense of accomplishment which comes from many hands working to a common end.

If you do try designing a large piece made up of separate squares, you may like to use the device I used on the carpet to conceal discrepancies in joining. The trick is to create a leafy border around the edge of each square which is busy enough to mask leaves not quite meeting at the edges, while breaking up the straight lines of the joins. Another tip is on the outer border where each side can be the same but turned around so that it does not look like a boring repeat. The outer border at the top and bottom of the

161

Cabbage and Apple Carpet have been omitted in the picture on the facing page, but they are reversed in the same way as the outer side borders.

Desportes' *Indian Hunter and Fisherman* (facing page) is a mate to his painting on page 134. To my delight I recently picked up an old Russian book on tapestries and found the extravagantly beautiful tapestry this cartoon had been made for.

The lover of decadence in me finds the ragged splits in the dynamic banana leaves and the brown weathering around the edges most appealing.

The grapevine curling up the trunk is one of the best leaf references in this book. Each leaf is so theatrically lit and full of colourful atmospheric changes. That persimmon-red into goldy-green leaf in the centre of the trunk could not fail to light up someone's needlepoint. There are even a few passion flowers lurking in the depths, and the melons are so succulent emerging from their leafy bed.

In the midst of all this wild sumptuousness, the two baskets are a beautiful excuse for a little still life. Each of these would make a gorgeous cushion design (see below).

The tapestry border (above) is from a series of tapestries illustrating the story of Joseph. Studying the borders you can see how differently the weavers interpreted each object. There are many similar subjects and figures but each piece of fruit or vegetable is so varied and fresh looking. Though the shading goes abruptly from darkest shadows to very bright highlights with simplified colouring, the essence of leaf and vegetable forms emerges.

As this tapestry border detail is laid out here, doesn't it suggest a marvellous window surround? I was bowled over by the idea of framing windows with needlepoint when I first went to Amsterdam and saw tapestry window pelmets made to look like *trompe-l'oeil* drapes with bowers of flowers.

Left and detail centre right: *The Indian Hunter and Fisherman* by Alexandre François Desportes (1661-1743), cartoon for the tapestry *Les Nouvelles Indes*, oil on canvas; Musée des Beaux-Arts, Marseilles.

Detail of border of tapestry illustrating the story of Joseph after a cartoon by Bronzino, Florentine Medici factory, mid-16th century; Palazzo Vecchio, Florence.

7 Flowers

Howern much I try I cannot seem to get very far from flowers in my decorative work. Just when I decide to do something sombre and mature in design, I stumble across a source dripping in flowers, and so deliriously enticing that I am seduced by this ephemeral theme all over again.

It is encouraging to see how even makers of fine silk carpets get totally carried away by naive flowers. This deliciously concocted Persian carpet (right) reminds me of those glass paperweights containing *millefiore*. Row upon row of childlike flat flowers make a confetti-filled world for daft cherubs to cavort in.

Even if you do not find this carpet at all to your taste you should learn a lot about witty, guileless composition from it. What about those borders – have you ever seen so much going on in one? The whole animal kingdom is there! I do hope it gives you a good chuckle and encourages jolly designs.

Marquetry is a favourite medium of mine despite the fact that it employs only a restricted palette of tones of browns. Mind you, there are quite a few shades, stretching from an ebony-brown background to the palest of amber tones, on Jan van Meeckeren's marquetry flowers (pages 166 and 167).

When I am forced to use a limited colour range for a kit, I often try to make it work in shades of grey or beige, then add enriching colours after the forms have been defined in monotone. It is amazing how very expressive a few tones can become and this

Detail of Kirman Lavere pictorial carpet, Persian, 1956.

White enamel étui decorated with flowers, Staffordshire, 18th century.

outstanding set of bouquets proves that point admirably. I am quite certain that Van Meeckeren worked harder at clarifying his shades than a painter would have using an array of colour. The more you look at the cabinet the more colourful it becomes.

Although Evelyn de Morgan's *Flora* (facing page) would not be considered a masterpiece, its breathtaking details are decorative gems. For instance, the ground is covered with jewel-like flowers on beautifully articulated grasses and leaves.

The pansy print on the dress would be an excellent inspiration for knitted motifs or for the background of a needlepoint. The red scarf with pungent pink and red roses is the rich punch that first caught my eye.

The seventeenth-century embroidered jacket (below right) is a wonderful swirl of flowers, leaves and birds. This fine all-over pattern, delineated with huge curlicues, has an entrancing delicacy.

Another beautiful colouring for delicate tones of flowers is the soft sage grey of the enamel étui (above left). The rich buttercup yellow, bright pink and royal blues really 'sing' on that soft grey green. The cake decoration swirls are delightfully frothy as a border.

The sheer force of brilliant red and yellow blooms (pages 170 and 171) should blow away for ever any 'delicate pastel' image of flowers that you may still cling to.

Notice how the stylized late seventeenth-century embroidered bloom

Previous page: Cabinet by Jan van Meeckeren, marquetry, circa 1709; Rijksmuseum, Amsterdam.

Above: Detail of flower motifs from *Flora* pictured on facing page.

Left: Margaret Laton jacket, linen embroidered with silks and silver-gilt thread, English, 1610-1630; V&A Museum, London.

Flora by Evelyn de
Morgan (1850–1919),
oil on canvas; de
Morgan Foundation,
London.

(facing page) juxtaposes a soft red and a mellow gold to strong effect. Whereas in Edward Burra's watercolour there is a more powerful contrast at play – strong scarlet red and deep yellows held in a grid of bottle-green foliage. The wreath of roses (facing page) also employs the strong contrast of saffron-yellow roses on dark green with deep blood-red roses.

Last year I was approached by Susan Lamb at my publishers with a commission to do a tapestry for one of their star writers, Ruth Rendell. At the same time Elian McCready, who has worked in my studio for some time, came in with a dynamic painting of pansies (page 172). I rang Ruth to ask what colours and themes she liked. She said there was pink in the house and, yes, she did like pansies.

We attacked the project with relish. Elian and I worked in three extra pansies from a Steve Lovi greeting card (page 172) to fill the space to overflowing. It is the deep dark pansy centres that make the composition thrilling. Often the darkness is doubly emphasized by the use of light gold or bright red at the edge to create exciting contrast. The raspberry-milk-shake-pink at the edges seemed the perfect colour with those hot oranges, cool lavender blues, and intense purple maroons.

Far left: Rug with sunflowers by Ashour Messelhi, 1983; collection of Ramses Wissa Wassef, Egypt.

Facing page

Silk embroidered panel from a box, English, late 17th century; V&A Museum, London.

Flower detail from *Pavots dans un vase bleu* by Kisling, oil on canvas, 1938. © ADAGP, Paris and DACS, London 1991.

Frontispiece to *Roses* by Mary Lawrence, engraving of a wreath of flowers, 1799.

Detail of *Flowers* by Edward Burra (1905-1976), watercolour of bouquet of flowers, painted circa 1964-1965.

Frontispiece

Above: *Pansies* by
Elian McCready,
watercolour, 1989.

Right: Still life of
pansies by Steve Lovi,
photograph, 1989.

The result you see here (facing page), has made my lecture audiences gasp with pleasure. So many requests came that Elian has developed a slightly simpler version of this tapestry as a kit (see page 191).

Because the shape of circular flowers satisfies something deep in me I have dedicated two pages to these lovely circular forms. As you can see (pages 174 and 175) they obviously inspire craftsmen and artists alike.

A painter whose colour has always astounded and delighted me is the French painter Redon. He was a mystic who did some of the most individual and moving flower studies in art.

Pansies by Kaffe
Fassett and Elian
McCready,
needlepoint panel kit
worked in long stitch
with wool yarns on
8-mesh canvas, 1989.

Fleurs by Odilon Redon (1840-1916), pastel.

A Young Daughter of the Picts by Jacques le Moyne de Morgues (circa 1533-1588), watercolour and gouache on vellum; Yale Center for British Art, New Haven, Connecticut, USA.

Supposedly, he painted nearly dead flowers because their colour had become so mysteriously intense and unusual.

Close examination shows Redon's pastel (above) to be almost crude in its simple, chalky strokes. I am sure it was done with great speed and excitement. The background smears of husky tones is worth the price of admission on their own! What a life he brings to scarlet terracotta and chestnut blue grey! Those dark aubergine flowers give a weighty depth to the higher colour and echo the charcoal shadows below.

Where would we be without a sense of humour? The older I get the louder and longer I laugh, sometimes to dispel the would-be heaviness that descends on the grown-ups! The competely delightfully decorated lady in

Facing page

Flowers in vase by Edith Pearson, needlepoint picture in tent stitch, 1772.

Hexagon patchwork, worked from various patterned fabrics, English, 19th century.

Paperweight, concentric millefiori with 'Clichy Rose', Clichy, French, circa 1845-55.

Louis XV enamelled gold snuffbox by M.R. Halle, Paris, mid-18th century.

Hayashi *cloisonné* vase, decorated with silver wire and enamel, Japanese, 19th century.

Floral beaded bag, French, circa 1900; Royal Ontario Museum, Toronto, Canada.

Detail of *A Still Life of a Primula* by Diderich (1816-1892), oil on canvas, 1854.

A Nurata Susani hanging, embroidery in silk on linen, Uzbekistan, 19th century.

Paperweight, factory unknown, French or Bohemian, circa 1845-55.

de Morgues' painting (page 174) is a perfect antidote to an over-serious world. She certainly is not afraid to celebrate what she has got!

The circular theme carries on with the eighteenth-century needlepoint (page 175). If this does not encourage the 'too-frightened-to-draw' brigade, nothing will. Look how each little element is so simple, yet how delightfully these childlike leaves and petals add up to a charming composition.

The Susani embroidery from Uzbekistan is one of the celebrated textiles that awoke my love of circles (see page 175). It has so many variations, yet each flower form uses the same flat colours, rather like paper cutouts.

As I was gathering material for this book I passed by the Japanese vase (page 175) several times as the entire piece is not to my taste. But when I looked closer, I was lost at once in the exquisite detail of each flower and leaf in such 'singing' colours.

Stripes conjure up an astonishingly fertile history. From ploughed fields to elegant brocades, the stripe has always been with us. When it comes to fabric design, examples are never-ending and even in porcelain we see a joyful use of decorative stripes.

The green burst on the Sèvres dish (facing page) would look wonderful as a needlepoint background with a pun-

A Group of Carnations from Thornton's *Temple of Flora*, hand-coloured engraving, circa 1800.

chy flower at its centre and bouquets in each of the big leaf forms. The cup and saucer are imitating fabric and have little blue flowers which almost get lost in the strong background.

The Minton passion flower jardinière (facing page) has a spirited high-summer colouring. The striped carnations from Thornton's *Temple of Flora* (above) make me think of smart British shirtmakers' shops.

Best of all though are the striped patches and chrysanthemum petals on the Japanese kimono. The arbitrary striped fabric patches tickle my surreal sense of design. How fresh, beautiful and amusing it is – I would love to have a shirt like this at once!

Facing page

Jardinière and underdish with pot-passion flower, Minton, English, 1858.

Plate and jug with flowers, Sèvres porcelain, French, mid-18th century.

Kimono with chrysanthemums and striped patches, silk, Japanese, late 19th century.

Porcelain cup and saucer with design of a contemporary fabric, Sèvres, French, 1766.

Although I am a sucker for fat, over-blown roses like those in the Berlin woolwork carpet (facing page), I am sure that many see them as common. But the operatic punch in them still attracts me. The leaves are so rounded and robust in their mossy tones.

One thing you can see in this needle-point which should be carefully avoided when designing is using the background black as a shadow tone in the leaves. It ends up looking more like a hole than a shadow.

Lauer's painting (right) shocked me when I first peered at a transparency of it under my magnifying glass. Though it appears at a distance to be a rich, thickly painted oil, it is in fact a water-colour. A more washy transparency is usually associated with this medium. These rich, dark colours really flow. The purple trumpet flowers and the intense yellow-orange nasturtiums are lovely. Even those whites glow with their grey shadows, and there is a great bloom on the grapes from the gold reflected light.

When I was young I used to be quite surprised when people got excited about musty old antiques. Threadbare carpets and brocades, peeling old murals, coroded tiles and pots seemed to send my mother's friends into raptures. Now I can see the charm in crumbling relics of another age. My house is full of cracked pots and worn-out carpets and I love them all with a passion.

There is a seductive mystery in sur-faces containing images that are partly disintegrated and distressed with dust.

Berlin woolwork carpet, embroidery worked with wool yarns, 19th century.

This Roman mosaic (page 180), for in-stance, is probably more beautiful today with its veil of obscurity than it was when new and clear. The flowers that are intact shine out, spotlit by the soft fading blooms around them.

Van der Ast's still life (page 181) is still clearly defined, but I know that the paint colours have mellowed mag-nificently since the seventeenth cen-tury when it was painted. There is something startling about the flowers. The tones of the top iris are more the colours of a rock, or a leaf, than a frail flower. I remember seeing such weird off-colourings on irises at the Chelsea Flower Show in London some twenty

A Still Life of Roses, Hyacinths and Grapes by Josef Lauer (1818-1881), watercolour.

179

years ago. They were the colour of old stained parchment with maroon veins. It was a ghostly beauty, indeed, as is that maroon-into-sky-blue iris with a rich gold tuft.

The amusing arrangement of dried flowers, grasses, stones and rolled paper (left) echoes the mellow colouring of the other works on these two pages. The teal-blue background works well with the powder pink, ochre grasses and dull red touches.

The idea for my *Flowers on Blue Marble* needlepoint (page 183) came originally from the Courbonne bouquet (page 182). I was attracted to the lavender pink of those roses against the tawny browns, mossy greens and

Above: Detail of floor mosaic with a basket of flowers, copy of original Roman mosaic, 2nd century AD; Museo Pio Clementino, Vatican.

Left: Picture made of dried flowers, grasses, stones, et cetera, English, 19th century; Hinton Ampner, Hampshire, England.

Facing page: *Irises, Roses, and other Flowers in a Porcelain Vase with Shells and a Beetle on a Table* by Balthasar van der Ast (circa 1590-1656), oil on canvas.

Roses, Convolvuli and other Flowers on a Ledge by Alexandre Courbonne (1792–1863), oil on canvas.

range of reds. The brilliant clarity of the fresh blue and white produced a good cutting sharpness in the centre, and the brown peacock butterfly (page 60) with his bold eyes related well to the circular auriculas.

To provide more edge to the bouquet the blue marble from an Italian tapestry (see detail right) replaced the soft golden-brown background of the painting. Stitching the marble was hugely enjoyable. I started at the top of the piece with four shades of blue. First I stitched the darkest inky blue in

Left: Detail of marble archway from a tapestry illustrating the story of Joseph, after a cartoon by Bronzino, Florentine Medici factory, mid-16th century; Palazzo Vecchio, Florence.

Facing page: *Flowers on Blue Marble* by Kaffe Fassett, needlepoint worked in tent stitch with wool yarns on 10-mesh canvas, 1990.

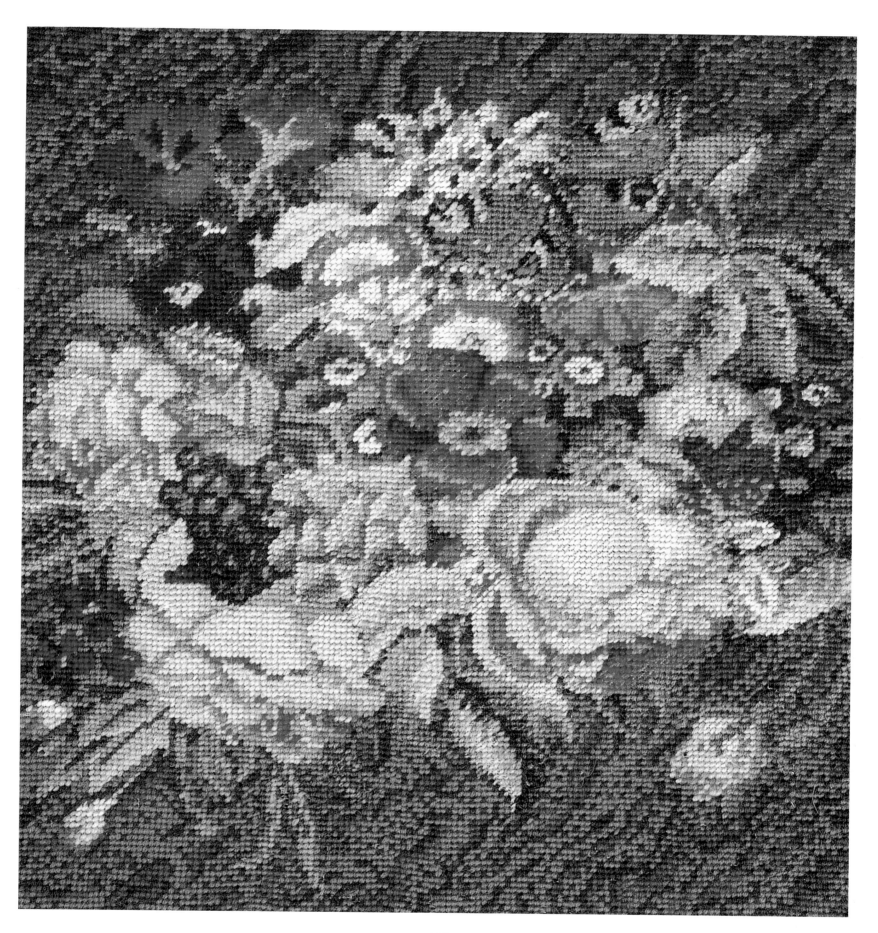

Detail of main well in Barlow showing unique use of whole flowers for 'well dressing'; Barlow, Derbyshire, England.

Micro-mosaic panel decorated with bunch of flowers, 20cm (8in) long, Italian, 19th century.

streaks and dots, then followed with the lightest tone, adding blue green for slight variation here and there, and finished by filling in with teal blue. At the bottom I reversed the teal and lightest grey blue.

From the tapestry border on page 22 I picked an artichoke, grapes and a pomegranate to add to my bouquet. By this example you can see how much you can change your original design source to suit your requirements. At a rough count there are about fifty colours in this needlepoint.

Being raised near Chinatown, San Francisco, I got used to seeing amazing amounts of red on red. I remember windows containing pyramids of oranges in turquoise bowls against red silk hangings with magenta fringes, and also children in pink shirts, red overalls, and brilliant red satin shoes with magenta and emerald flower embroidery on them.

Later, I discovered that wonderful painting by Matisse of a red studio containing many red objects. The Tibetans and South Americans love mixtures of red and plummy pinks, as do the Indians and Moroccans.

These pages (184 and 185) are a celebration of reds. Even in tasteful restrained England I found this well dressing which shoved crimson,

Flowers from *The Japanese Tattoo* by Sandi Fellman, 1986.

Red Chair by Kaffe Fassett, needlepoint chair cover worked in tent stitch with wool yarns on 8-mesh canvas, 1989.

magenta and maroon together like there was no tomorrow! This unique British custom, found in Derbyshire, of embedding flower-petals and leaves into clay on the county's wells is a delight. This one with its stone separations looks as playful as a Matisse paper cutout. It uses whole flowers, berries and straw to juicy effect.

The Italian micro-mosaic (facing page) is more restrained in its use of materials – tiny pieces of glass – but just as flamboyant in its use of colour. The faded wine-coloured pink and dark rust-red carnation make a winning combination.

The *Red Chair* needlepoint (above) arose from a commission that required 'a dash of red in the house'. Back came my childhood memories of magenta fringe, oranges and red silk. The flowers came from many Oriental sources including a Japanese floral tattoo (above left). Each petal and leaf in the tent stitch embroidery is outlined in a bright light colour like high lime green, yellow, or sky blue, and then shaded away.

When you want jewel-bright colours to really sing out there is nothing quite like black as a base. What attracted me to Johann Baptist Drechsler's voluptuous bouquet (right) is the vibration between the intense royal blues and vibrant orangey reds. Each flower is stunningly three-dimensional, making it easy to translate into needlepoint.

It is interesting to note what a wide range of contrast there is in this late eighteenth-century painting, from the whitest highlights to shadowy forms that are virtually black. The largest area of the painting uses deep full-blooded colours with dark glorious shadows.

In my *Bouquet on Black* needlepoint chair cover (facing page), which I designed for a Paris shop, I used a wide range of contrast but no sharp white. The shop that the chair went to has a carpet of off-white dots on black, so I used that as a base. The dark plums, auriculas and pansies almost merge with the black ground creating mysterious corners for the bouquet. While stitching the work, some leaves got so dark that they actually did start to disappear, so I introduced a silver reverse side or placed a brilliant orange nasturtium under dark leaves.

The flowers and fruit come from dozens of different design sources, and six stitchers with their individual approaches worked on the needlepoint. Some of the sources are from paintings, many like Johann Baptist

Bouquet on Black by Kaffe Fassett, needlepoint chair cover worked in tent stitch with wool yarns on 8-mesh canvas, 1990.

Drechsler's *Flowers in a Sculptured Vase* (above). The hollyhock is a rendering of a sixteenth-century hollyhock watercolour by Jacques le Moyne de Morgues. Thoughtfully mixing mid-nineteenth-century with mid-sixteenth-century painted flowers works quite successfully.

Coming to the end of my collection of sources, I hope that it has tapped your flow of creative ideas. Here's to your confident expression!

Flowers in a Sculptured Vase by Johann Baptist Drechsler (1756-1811), oil on canvas.

ere are some helpful and flexible basic guidelines for working the types of needlepoints featured in this book. They are included to refresh the memories of those of you who have not picked up your needle for a few years and to show the beginner how simple canvaswork really is.

If you are a beginner, don't hesitate to have a go! You will pick up needlepoint methods by just getting on with it and learning by your mistakes. If the technicalities start to get in my way, I bend the rules to facilitate the creative flow of improvisation. Always keep in mind that the emotional impact of colour and pattern is the top priority.

Needlepoint Canvas

Needlepoint is worked on an evenweave canvas. The canvas comes in various mesh sizes, ranging from the finest with 32 holes or threads per 2.5cm (1in) to the largest with 3 holes per 2.5cm (1in). The finer meshes are used for the tiny stitches of *petit point* and the bigger for carpets. I generally prefer using a 10-mesh or a slightly larger 8-mesh canvas. These two mesh sizes give me a stitch size that is small enough to create the detail I want but big enough for my stitching to proceed rapidly.

Apart from coming in different mesh sizes, the canvas also comes in three different types – mono (or single-thread) canvas, interlocked canvas, and double-thread (or Penelope) canvas. It is largely a case of personal taste which type of canvas you choose to work with. If you are doing *petit point*, mono canvas is a must because it is the only type that comes in the finer mesh sizes from 32- to 16-mesh.

I like working with double-thread canvas, because you can work all types of stitches on it, including half cross stitch. Also with double-thread canvas, the threads can be split apart in areas so that it converts to mono canvas. In this way fine stitches for details can be combined on the same canvas with larger stitches for backgrounds, for instance. Double-thread canvas is usually softer, too, because it has not been stiffened as much and the individual threads are finer than the individual threads of a mono canvas of the same gauge.

Interlocked canvas is stiffer, but because the threads are locked together it does not fray as easily or distort during stitching as much as the other types.

When buying canvas for a project remember to allow for at least 5cm (2in) extra unworked canvas all around the design.

Yarns

You will need a yarn that is thick enough to cover the canvas threads. The standard wool needlepoint yarns come in three thicknesses – crewel, tapestry and Persian.

Crewel wool is quite fine and at least three strands together are needed for a 10-mesh canvas. It is perfect for mixing your own tones and colours, when you cannot find a thicker single strand of the shade you are searching for. Just thread together a strand each of two or three different colours of crewel yarn close to the shade required.

Tapestry wool is thicker than crewel, and a single strand will usually cover a 10-mesh canvas. Two strands of tapestry yarn are needed for a 7 or 8-mesh canvas.

Persian wool is made up of three strands of yarn that can be easily separated. Spun slightly more tightly than tapestry wool, although of a similar thickness, Persian wool gives a lovely texture to fringes on needlepoint carpets.

Needlepoint Stitches

There are many types of stitches which have been developed for needlepoint. Generally I work in tent stitch or random long stitch, because they are quick and easy and give the type of texture I like for my designs.

Personally, I like working needlepoint handheld, because I find it easier to manipulate and because I can then carry my work with me wherever I go. You may, however, find it more to your taste to work with an embroidery frame because it leaves two hands free, and also keeps the embroidery from being distorted if you tend to stitch too tightly. Try it both ways!

The three most popular techniques for forming tent stitch are called continental, basketweave, and half cross. They all look the same from the front, and I use them alternately as the fancy takes me, even on the same canvas! (For pale, solid backgrounds, however, it is best to stick to one type of stitch to avoid creating ridges on the right side of the work.)

The instructions for only half cross tent stitch and continental tent stitch are given here, as they are more suited to the use of a wide range of colours and are much easier to learn than basketweave.

Continental Tent Stitch

Continental tent stitch forms long, slanted stitches on the reverse and can be worked on any type of needlepoint canvas. Before beginning, choose a blunt-ended tapestry needle, large enough to hold the yarn without damaging it, but not so large that it has to be forced through the canvas.

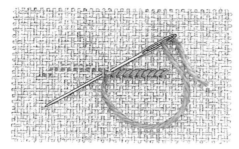

1. When beginning, leave a 2.5cm (1in) long loose end at the back and work the first few stitches from right to left over it, as shown here.

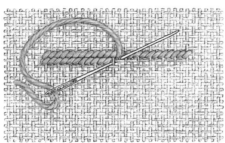

2. Work the following row of stitches below the last row. Continue working alternately from right to left, then from left to right.

Half Cross Stitch

The half cross stitch technique uses less yarn than the other two tent stitch techniques. This is because the stitches at the back of the work are short, vertical stitches that do not cover the back of the canvas. When an entire design is worked in half cross stitch the resulting needlepoint is not as thick as a needlepoint worked in basketweave or continental tent stitch. Half cross stitch cannot be worked on mono canvas. It requires a double-thread or interlocked canvas.

Work in rows alternately from left to right and right to left, making short vertical stitches at the back as shown here. When ending a length of yarn, pass it through a few stitches at the back or merely catch it into the next row.

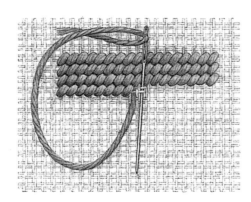

Random Long Stitch

This stitch is fabulous for filling in large areas of background fast! Or even for working entire, large needlepoint wall hangings (see pages 8-9 and page 11).

Make sure you use a double-thread canvas and a thick enough strand of yarn to cover the canvas threads. For some mesh sizes a single strand of tapestry wool is almost thick enough, but not quite, and two strands of tapestry wool together is just too bulky. In such a case try adding a single strand of crewel yarn or, if necessary, two strands of crewel yarn.

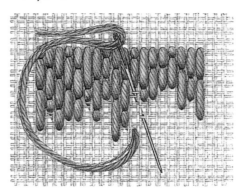

The random long stitch should be worked in varying lengths along each row. Work one row from right to left, then the following row from left to right, and so on alternately.

Blocking and Sizing

Once you have learnt random long stitch or traditional tent stitch you can let your fingers do the stitching and concentrate on lovely colours and beautiful designs.

While working your needlepoint, do not worry if it seems to become slightly distorted. The wool yarns are very amenable to being flattened and straightened into shape after the work has been completed by dampening and stretching.

To block the finished needlepoint, place it face down on a board and dampen it thoroughly by spraying it with water, or using a damp cloth or sponge. Then nail it into shape following your original design for the size guide, and placing the nails about 3cm (1¼in) apart along each side. Allow the needlepoint to dry completely before removing, even if it takes several days.

You can use a wallpaper paste to fix the shape if desired. It will give the needlepoint more body and resilience. Always check the contents of the paste, however, to make sure it will not damage the needlepoint fibres. If a frame has been used, paste may not be needed.

Illustration Credits

The author and publisher would like to thank all of the museums and collections named in the captions for their permission to reproduce illustrations. In addition, they would like to thank the following museums, collections and photographic libraries who are not acknowledged in the captions.

Aberdeen Art Gallery and Museums, Aberdeen City Arts Department: p.130 *top right*.

American Museum of Natural History, New York; courtesy of the Department of Library Services, Tr. 2821(3): p.74 (photo O. Bauer & J. Beckett).

Archer Art, Amsterdam: p.119 *top*.

Bridgeman Art Library, London: p.2 (Roy Miles Fine Paintings, London), pp.56–57, p.60 *bottom left*, p.61, p.73 (Johnny van Haeften, London), p.78 *bottom* (David Messum Fine Paintings), p.79, p.81 *top right* (Oscar & Peter Johnson Ltd, London) *and bottom*, p.89, p.91 *bottom left*, p.95 *top left* (Roy Miles Fine Paintings, London), p.99, p.100 (Giraudon), p.102, p.107 *middle left and bottom left*, p.124, p.126 *bottom left*, p.127 *top* (Josef Mensing Gallery, Hamm-Rhynern), p.128 *top* (Bonhams, London), p.130 *bottom right*, pp.134–135 (Giraudon), p.137 *bottom left* (Giraudon), *top right and middle left*, p.142, p.158 *top left* (Agnew & Sons, London), p.162 (Giraudon), p.163 *centre* (Giraudon), p.168 *top right and bottom right*, p.169, p.177, p.182 *top*.

British Library (India Office Library), London: p.62 *bottom*, p.75 *top right*, p.86 *top*, p.96, p.107 *top left*, p.127 *bottom*.

Christie's, London: p.24 *top left*, pp.38–39, p.50 *top and bottom*, p.51 *bottom*, p.55, p.60 *top right, middle centre and bottom centre*, p.64 *bottom left*, p.65 *bottom*, p.68 *top*, p.90 *top right and bottom left*, p.97 *top*, p.107 *top right and bottom right*, p.117, p.122 *top left*, p.144 *bottom right*, p.147, p.148 *bottom right*, p.157, p.158 *top right*, pp.164–165, p.168 *top left*, p.171 *bottom left*, p.174 *top left*, p.175 *top centre, middle left, middle centre and middle right*, p.176 *top left and bottom right*, p.181, p.184 *right*.

Christie's, New York: p.32.

Corning Museum of Glass, Corning, New York: p.175 *bottom left and bottom right*.

Ehrman, London: p.78 *top*, p.106 (photo Henry Bourne).

E.T. Archive, London: p.60 *bottom right*, p.69 *bottom*, p.116 *bottom left*, p.143, p.170 *top left*, p.171 *top right*, p.178 (Mayorcas Ltd, London).

Fine Art Photographic Library Ltd, London: p.28, p.33 *top*, pp.42–43, p.60 *middle left* (Anthony Mitchell Paintings, Nottingham), p.81 *top left*, p.90 *bottom right*, p.107 *middle right*, p.110 *middle right*, pp.112–113, p.129 *top*, p.130 *top left and middle left*, p.158 *bottom* (Burlington Paintings, London), p.175 *top right*, p.179 (Hamm-Rhynern Gallery), p.187.

Werner Forman Archive, London: p.25 *bottom left*, p.95 *top right*, p.145 *top left*, p.170 *bottom*, p.176 *bottom left*.

Glasgow Museums and Art Galleries (The Burrell Collection), Glasgow, Scotland: p.82 *top*.

Sonia Halliday Photographs: p.93, p.119 *bottom*.

Iona Antiques, London: p.110 *bottom left*.

Lefevre Gallery, London: p.171 *bottom right*.

Mallett & Son (Antiques) Ltd, London: p.24 *top right and bottom right*, p.25 *top left*, p.29, p.33 *bottom*, p.62 *top*, p.95 *bottom left*, p.97 *middle and bottom*, p.175 *top left*.

Metropolitan Museum of Art, New York; A.W. Bahr Collection, Fletcher Fund, 1947: p.116 *top left*.

Metropolitan Museum of Art, New York; Gift of Henry G. Marquand, 1894: p.118 *right*. Metropolitan Museum of Art, New York; Rogers Fund, 1916: p.87.

National Gallery of Art, Washington; Gift of Edgar William and Bernice Chrysler Garbisch: pp.120–121.

National Trust Photographic Library, London: p.137 *middle centre* (photo J. Bethell), p.180 *bottom* (photo Nick Carter).

The Royal Collection, London; Reproduced by gracious permission of Her Majesty the Queen: p.110 *bottom right*.

The Royal Danish Collections at Rosenborg Castle, Copenhagen: p.122 *top right* (photo Lennart Larsen).

Royal Horticultural Society, Lindley Library, London: p.148 *bottom left and top*.

Royal Ontario Museum; Gift of Mrs. W.D. Ross: p.175 *bottom centre*.

The Fine Arts Museums of San Francisco, Achenbach Foundation for Graphic Arts purchases: p.95 *bottom right*, p.123, p.128 *bottom*.

Scala, Florence: endpapers, p.10 *middle and bottom*, pp.16–17, p.18, pp.20–21, p.22, p.25 *bottom right*, pp.26–27, p.31, p.41 *top left*, p.46, p.48, pp.52–53, p.58, p.59, p.60 *top centre*, p.75 *left*, pp.76–77, pp.84–85, p.92, pp.104–105, p.110 *top right*, p.115, p.116 *top right*, p.119 *middle*, p.125, p.137 *top left, top centre, middle right and bottom centre*, pp.138–139, p.140, p.144 *top left, top right and bottom left*, p.145 *top right, bottom left and bottom right*, pp.152–153, p.159 *top*, p.163 *top*, p.180 *top*, p.182 *bottom*.

Brian Schuel Collection, London: p.184 *left*.

Science Photo Library, London: p.19 *bottom left* (photo Sinclair Stammers), p.19 *bottom right* (photo Patricia Tye).

Sotheby's, London: p.86 *bottom*, p.91 *top left*, p.137 *bottom right*, p.155, p.176 *top left*.

Yale Centre for British Art, New Haven, Connecticut; Paul Mellon Collection: p.174 *right*.

Photographers' Credits

The author and publisher would like to acknowledge the following photographers.

Jonathon Bosley: p.161.

David Cripps: p.3, pp.8–9, p.11 *top and bottom*, p.12, p.13, p.14 *top and bottom*, p.15, p.24 *bottom left*, p.25 *top right*, p.40, p.44, p.47, p.51 *top*, p.63 *bottom*, pp.66–67, p.69 *top*, p.82 *bottom*, p.88, p.91 *top right*, p.94, p.101, p.108, p.111 *top left*, p.118 *left*, p.129 *bottom*, p.131, p.141, p.151, p.160, p.172 *top*, p.173, p.183, p.185 *right*, p.186.

Chris Drake: p.111 *top right*.

Roy Fox: p.30, pp.34–35, p.41 *all illustrations except top left*, p.54, p.60 *middle right*, p.64 *top left and top right*, p.65 *top*, p.68 *bottom*, p.72 *top and bottom*, p.130 *middle right*.

Walter Gardiner Photography: p.83.

Steve Lovi: p.146 *top*, p.172 *bottom*.

Duncan MacQueen: p.36, p.37 *bottom*.

Daniel McGrath for V&A Museum, London: p.171 *top left*.

Christine Smith for V&A Museum, London: p.98 *bottom right*, p.126 *top left*, p.148 *middle left*.

Ole Woldeye: p.156.

Most of the Kaffe Fassett needlepoint and knitting designs that appear in this book are available as kits.

To order the kits featured in the book or to obtain a complete list of Kaffe Fassett kits contact either Ehrman or Rowan Yarns (addresses below).

Ehrman Kits
The following needlepoint and knitting kits which appear in this book are available from Ehrman:

Needlepoint
Unless otherwise stated, all of the needlepoint kits are suitable as cushions or pictures, i.e. approximately 36–38cm (14–15in) square.

page 12 *Rose and Ribbon*
page 15 *Autumn Roses*
page 63 *Hawk Moth*
pages 66–67 *Lizard Panel*
page 69 *Turtle*
page 91 *Red Parrots*
page 106 *Rooster Cushion*
page 108 *Japanese Rooster and Hen*
page 111 *Bulldog*
page 118 *Pansy the Cow*
page 129 *Rabbits*
page 151 *Artichoke*
page 160 *Cabbage and Apple Carpet*
page 173 *Pansies Panel*

Knitting
page 25 *Marble Blocks Sweater*
page 45 *Fish and Waves Waistcoat*
page 78 *Leopardskin Sweater*
page 88 *Parrot Sweater*
page 141 *Fossil Jacket*

Ehrman Addresses
For details of stockists and mail order sources of Ehrman kits, please write or contact the following distributors:

United Kingdom: Ehrman, 14/16 Lancer Square, Kensington Church Street, London W8 4EP. Tel: (071) 937 4568

USA: Ehrman, 5 Northern Boulevard, Amherst, NH 03031. Tel: (603) 886 5041

Australia: Sunspun Enterprises Pty Ltd, 195 Canterbury Road, Canterbury, Victoria 3126. Tel: (03) 830 1609

Canada: Cruickshanks, 1015 Mount Pleasant Road, Toronto M4P 2MI. Tel: (416) 488 8292

Italy: Sybilla S.r.l., Via Rizzoli 7, 40125 Bologna. Tel: (051) 750 875

France: Armada, Collonge, Lournand, 71250 Cluny. Tel: 85 59 1356

New Zealand: Quality Handcrafts, PO Box 1486, Auckland.

Sweden: UTILIA, Box 2055, S-103 12 Stockholm. Tel: (468) 103355

Rowan Yarns Kits
The following knitting kit which appears in this book is available from Rowan Yarns:
page 24 *Tumbling Blocks Sweater*

Rowan Yarns Addresses
For details of stockists and mail order sources of Rowan kits, please write or contact the following distributors:

United Kingdom: Rowan Yarns, Green Lane Mill, Holmfirth, West Yorkshire, England HD7 1RE. Tel: (0484) 681881

USA: Westminster Trading Corporation, 5 Northern Boulevard, Amherst, NH 03031. Tel: (603) 886 5041

Australia: Rowan (Australia), 191 Canterbury Road, Canterbury 3126, Victoria. Tel: (03) 830 1609

Belgium: Hedera, Deistsesstraat 172, B-3030 Leuven. Tel: (016) 232189

Canada: Estelle Designs and Sales Ltd, 38 Continental Place, Scarborough, Ontario M1R 2TA. Tel: (416) 298 9922

Denmark: Designer Garn, Aagade 3, Roerbaek, DK 9500 Hobro. Tel: (098) 557 811

Finland: Helmi Vuorelma-Oy, Vesijarven Katu 13, SF-15141 Lahti. Tel: 18 268 31

Holland: Henk & Henrietta Beukers, Dorpsstraat 9, 5327 Ar Hurwenen. Tel: (04182) 1764

Iceland: Stockurinn, Orlygsdottir, Kjorgardi, Laugavegi 59, 101 Reykjavik. Tel: (91) 182 58

Italy: La Compagnia del Cotone, Via Mazzini 44, 10123 Torino. Tel: (011) 878 381

Japan: Diakeito Co Ltd, 1-5-23 Nakatsu Kita-Ku, Osaka 531. Tel: (06) 371 5657

Mexico: Estambresy Tejidos Finos S.A.D.C.V., A.V. Michoacan 30-A, Local 3 Esq Av Mexico, Col Hipodromo Condesa 06170, Mexico 11. Tel: 2 64 84 74

New Zealand: Creative Fashion Centre, PO Box 45083, Epuni Railway, Lower Hutt. Tel: (04) 674 085

Norway: Eureka, PO Box 357, 1401 Ski. Tel: (09) 871 909

Singapore: Classical Hobby House, 1 JLN Anak Bukit, No B2-15 Bukit Timah Plaza, Singapore 2158. Tel: 4662179

Sweden: Wincent, Luntmakargatan 56, 113 58 Stockholm. Tel: (08) 327 060

This book has taken a long time to evolve and is the joyful and dedicated team work of editor Sally Harding, designer Polly Dawes and picture researcher Mary Jane Gibson. Each of their inputs was inspired and their encouragement invaluable, so gratitude in abundance!

Thanks also to David Cripps for cheerfully and beautifully photographing our stitched examples and the opening chapter.

And thank you to Steve Lovi for contributing his handsome still life of pansies (page 172) and for the tireless encouragement he gives so generously.

Thank you indeed to Hugh Ehrman for producing and marketing the new kits inspired by this book.

Waves of affectionate thanks to my magnificent studio crew – who stitched and knitted valiantly to complete work for the book: Maria Brannan, David Forrest, Jill Gordon, Elian McCready, Francesca Nurse and Caroline Robins. For keeping the studio joyously afloat through chaotic times my secretary Juliana Yeo gets my thanks. And as always many thanks to Richard Womersley for his calm support.

Lastly thanks to Sarah Wallace at Century who enthusiastically believed in this book and got it started and to Hilary Arnold for picking up the ball and running with it.

Index